REMEMBERING

GALESBURG

REMEMBERING GALESBURG

TOM WILSON

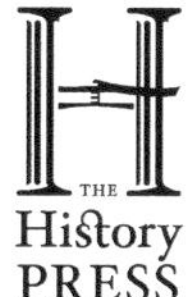

Published by The History Press
Charleston, SC 29403
www.historypress.net

All images courtesy of Galesburg Public Library unless otherwise noted.

First published 2009
Second printing 2009
Third printing 2012

Manufactured in the United States

ISBN 978.1.59629.673.2

Library of Congress Cataloging-in-Publication Data

Wilson, Tom, 1938-
Remembering Galesburg / Tom Wilson.
p. cm.
ISBN 978-1-59629-673-2
1. Galesburg (Ill.)--History. 2. Galesburg (Ill.)--Social life and customs. 3. Knox County (Ill.)--History, Local. I. Title.
F549.G15.W65 2009
977.3'49--dc22
2009008965

Notice: The information in this book is true and complete to the best of our knowledge. It is offered without guarantee on the part of the author or The History Press. The author and The History Press disclaim all liability in connection with the use of this book.

CONTENTS

PREFACE

The contained historical stories have been chosen from a weekly column entitled "Tracking History" in the *Galesburg Register-Mail* newspaper. The series began in 2004 and has been derived from data in newspapers dating from the late 1800s forward. Many of the incidents have been experienced by yours truly and contain a multitude of memories. Readers of the column have contributed additional information and suggested topics for many of the articles.

Although the majority of the columns have concentrated on Galesburg, Illinois, there are many that cover past history in Knox County and the communities of Abingdon, Knoxville, Oneida and Monmouth, just to name a few. Due to Galesburg's relationship with the Quad-Cities and Peoria, historical stories that pertain to these areas are also included.

Column subject matter has included the area's relationship with Superman, poet Carl Sandburg, President Ronald Reagan, President Ford's mother, comedian W.C. Fields, Mother Burg Salve, the O.T. Johnson Big Store, Mother Bickerdyke, sports, bears, dogs, ice cream, railroads, dandelions, famous musicians, fires, elephants and magic. Some of the columns are educational, some are funny, some are sad and a few are almost unbelievable. An attempt has been made to include something for everyone's taste and interest.

Yours truly is a lifetime resident of Galesburg, Illinois, and has been married to Judy, a retired schoolteacher, for nearly fifty years. Past professional experiences have included being a radio news director, elected municipal treasurer, executive director of a downtown business association, sports announcer and even a newspaper carrier boy. I have served as a trustee of Carl Sandburg Community College, president of the Illinois Community College Trustees Association, president of the Illinois Downtown Association and state vice-president of the Illinois Jaycees.

Some wise old philosopher once said, "If we don't study our past, we will be doomed to repeat it." I don't believe repeating it would be such a bad thing.

ACKNOWLEDGEMENTS

The surprise opportunity to have my *Register-Mail* history columns published in book form would not have occurred without the help and understanding of a very special group of individuals.

In particular, my gratitude is extended to Sue Davidson for her sincere interest, understanding, editing and technical assistance in submitting the contents for publication. Thanks to Galesburg Library archivist Patty Mosher for helping to choose and prepare book photos.

Thank you to Tom Martin, editor of the *Register-Mail*, who originally presented the opportunity to publish my historical columns in the newspaper. Thank you to former publisher Don Cooper, current publisher Tony Scott, Jay Redfern, Rob Buck, Mike Homco, Jane Carlson, John Pulliam, Jeff Holt, Bill Gaither, Kent Kriegshauser and Ken Exum, who as *Register-Mail* staff members have made my task possible.

A special thank-you to Jonathan Simcosky of The History Press, who has literally carried me through the process of having my history columns published in book form.

Last, but not least, thank you to my wife Judy for her patience, understanding and confidence extended to me during this project.

CHAPTER I

GALESBURG AND KNOX COUNTY

A Humble Beginning for Knox County

In 1828, a voyager named Daniel Robertson left his home in the east and eventually reached what is now Henderson, Illinois, in the northern section of the current Knox County. Robertson marked his place in history by building a home shelter and thus became the first white man to settle in what would become Knox County.

Other settlers followed close behind, arriving from Virginia, Kentucky and the Carolinas. As the others arrived, they found great timbers and fertile plains, built shelters and thus a new Illinois civilization begun. The parade of hearty souls included Jacob Gum, a Baptist minister who preached the first sermon in the county. Into the settlement was born the first white child to Mrs. Zephaniah Gum. The first death among the early settlers was seventeen-year-old Phillip Nance. Nance is buried in a lone grave on farmland six miles north of Galesburg.

The settlement grew rapidly in size and numbers made it necessary to form a county government. Henderson, currently located north of Galesburg, became a thriving trading post and served as the unofficial county seat for one year. The village included five stores, three wagon factories, a blacksmith shop, a gristmill and even a distillery. The population reached a peak of one thousand residents for a short time. It should be noted that there were originally two areas known as Henderson. One was the early settlement north of Galesburg and the other, named Henderson Town, was eventually changed to Knoxville in 1837.

When Knox County was first incorporated it was connected with Fulton County for judicial and governmental purposes. Knoxville became the first official county seat. Many of the early settlers who lived in Henderson

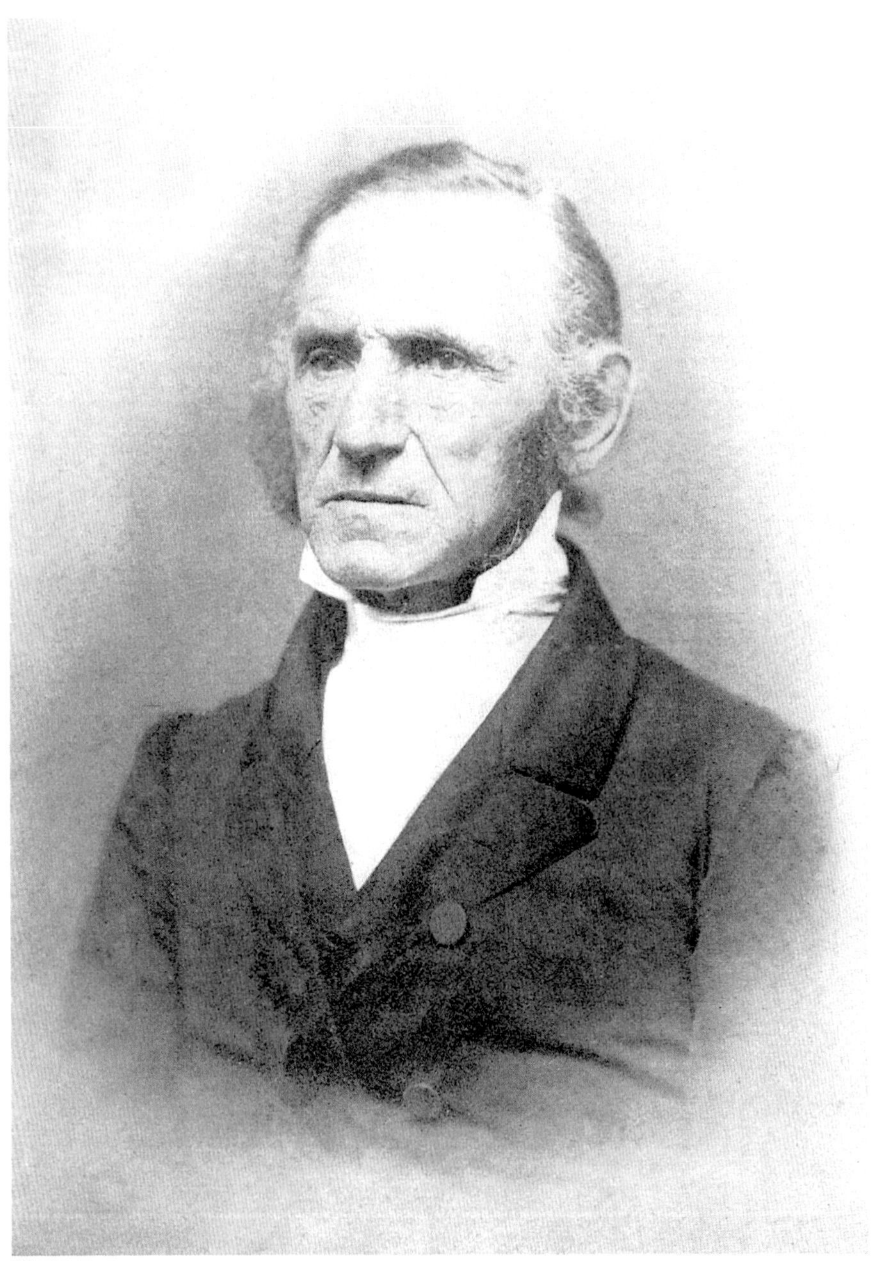

George Washington Gale, founder of Galesburg.

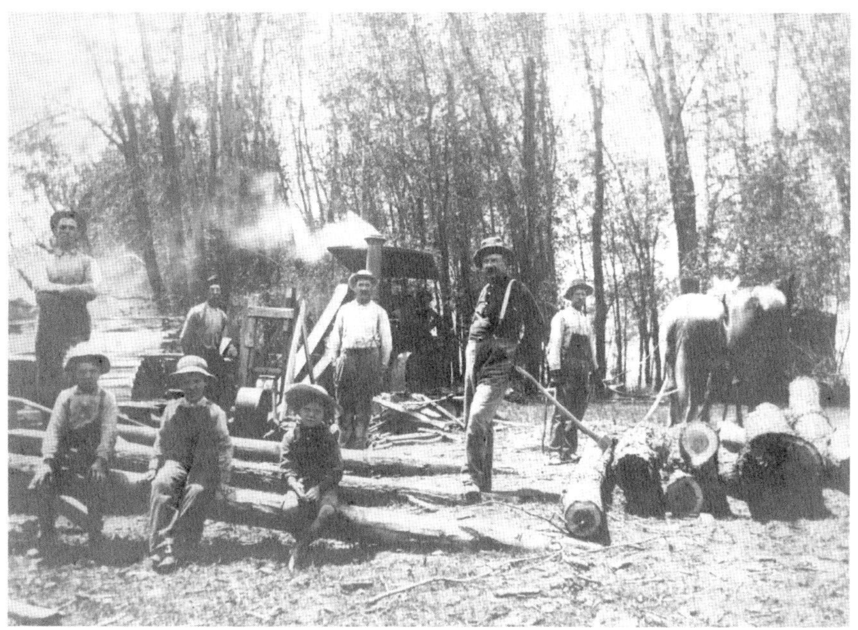

An early sawmill north of Galesburg, 1900.

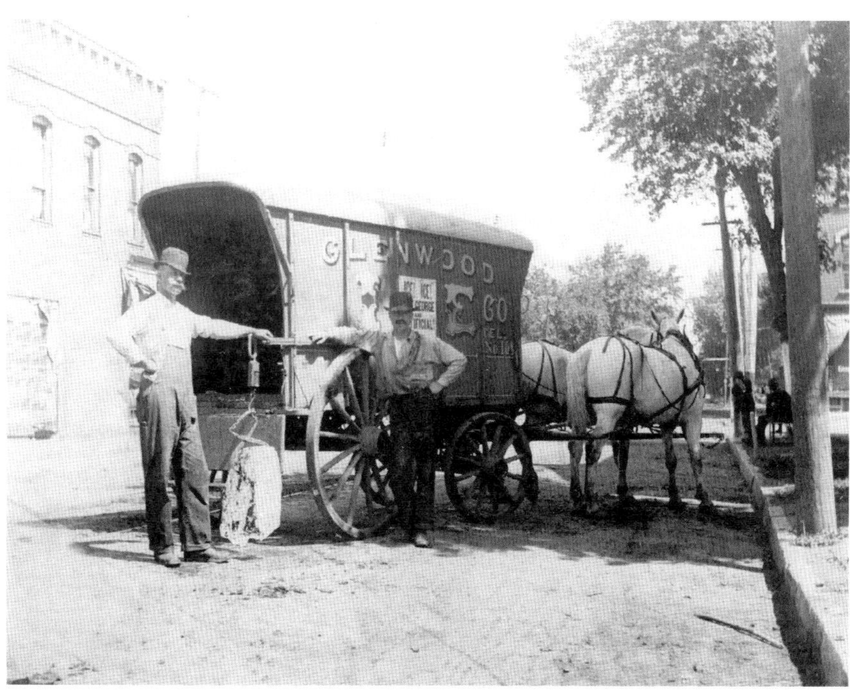

The horse-drawn ice wagon of Glenwood Ice Co., 1900.

moved to Knoxville and created an angling road laid out between the two communities. The first state road laid out in what is now Knox County began in Vandalia, passed through the eastern portion of the county and ended in Galena. There was no bridge over the Spoon River until 1839; thus, the river was either forded or ferried.

In 1836, a multitude of additional settlers moved into the county from the east. The largest colony coming from New York founded what is now Galesburg and established Knox College. Knox County was first laid out into sixteen townships. It was not until 1841 that complete legal records began to be kept when Stephen A. Douglas arrived in Knoxville to preside over the district court.

Rapid changes occurred when a new-fangled contraption called a railroad slowly made its way west from Chicago. When the railroad originally reached the vicinity of Wataga, it was the intention to turn west through Henderson and onto the Mississippi River. This all changed abruptly when a fellow named Gale donated land farther south; this was the beginning of the end for the continued growth of Henderson and Knoxville and an added beginning for Galesburg.

Incidentally, Knox County, Illinois, was named in honor of General Henry Knox. The general was originally an American bookseller from Boston and became chief of artillery for the Revolutionary army and later secretary of war in President George Washington's first cabinet. Henry Knox appeared to be a "designated" person to have places named after him. Forts in Kentucky and Maine were named in his honor, along with counties in Indiana, Kentucky, Maine, Missouri, Nebraska, Ohio, Tennessee and Texas. As an added touch, Knoxville, Tennessee, is also named for him.

FOUNDERS REMEMBERED

The last surviving colonist who helped lay the foundation of Galesburg passed away on January 16, 1928. Mrs. Clarison Root Hinckley of 657 North Kellogg Street was the daughter of Riley Root. She arrived in August 1836 at the age of four with her father, as part of the original thirty-nine colonists at Log City near the current site of Lake Storey.

Mrs. Hinckley had been the oldest surviving Knox College student, graduating in 1845. Riley Root helped build the first house in Galesburg and was credited with inventing the original railroad snowplow in 1855. Clarison Root Hinckley moved to the site that is now Galesburg in 1837. She celebrated her ninety-sixth birthday just prior to her death.

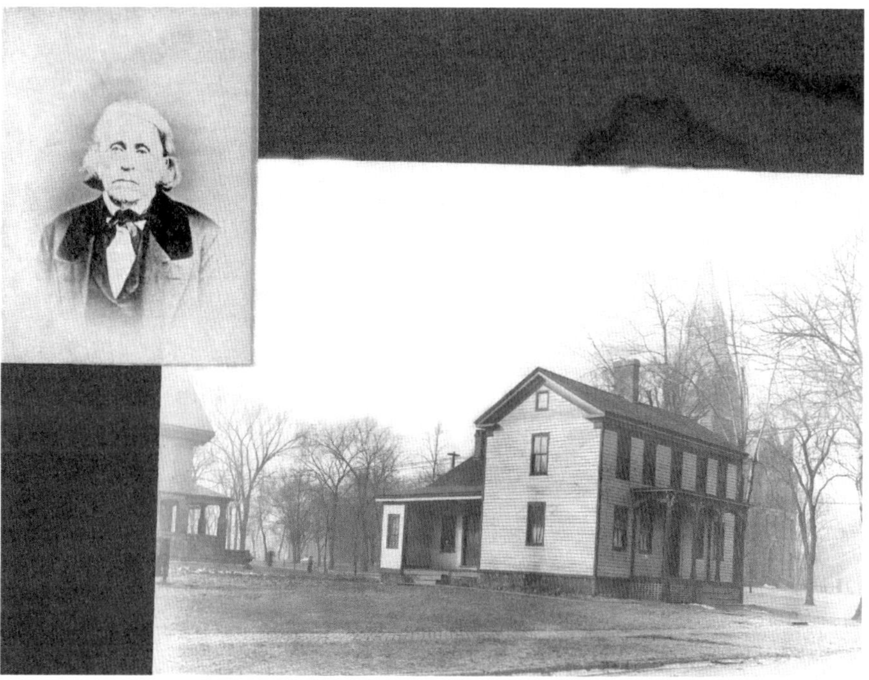

The residence of Sylvanus Ferris, one of the early founders of Galesburg and Knox College, 1800.

Samuel W. May, inventor of the May Windmill, passed away at his home in Rio, Illinois, on March 18, 1918, at the age of eighty-two. Sam arrived with his parents at Log City, where his father Harvey built the first log cabin. Harvey would eventually place the building on skids and, with ten yoke of oxen, hauled the structure to Galesburg. Harvey May started a factory in Galesburg and invented the first steel plow used in Knox County. Samuel May attended Knox College and joined his father's business. He would eventually engage in farming near Rio, raising cattle and hogs on his five-hundred-acre property. The first two hundred windmills invented by Samuel were made on the farm.

Chiffoenette Tompkins Ward Jones passed away on October 2, 1925. Her father, Samuel Tompkins, was one of the original colonists of Galesburg and was instrumental in starting the Knox Academy, which became Knox College. Chiffoenette attended the academy for two years; however, her father did not believe in higher education for girls and thus she did not graduate from Knox College.

Tompkins Street in Galesburg, where the family residence was located, was named in honor of Samuel. Chiffoenette's second marriage was to Daniel Jones, who farmed west of Galesburg. A son Carlos and grandson Horace were graduates of the college founded by her father. Mrs. Jones was a descendant of Captain James Cudworth, who came over on the historic vessel the *Mayflower*. She was active in the Daughters of the American Revolution and the Baptist Church while residing in Galesburg.

Martha Hitchcock, granddaughter of G.W. Gale, who founded Galesburg, passed away in August 1966 at the age of ninety-seven. Galesburg history ran in her bloodline in numerous ways. Martha's father, Henry E. Hitchcock, had a local school named in his honor. Her grandfather, Reverend George Washington Gale, founded the city, Knox College and later had a factory named in his honor.

Reverend Gale's daughter, Margaret, married Hitchcock, who was a member of the first graduating class at Knox. Hitchcock became a professor of mathematics at Knox College and became chancellor of the University of Nebraska. Martha Hitchcock, who never married, last visited Galesburg in the mid-'50s.

Death notices pertaining to the descendants of those who founded Galesburg, Illinois, often educate us on the rich history of the community. A trip through Hope Cemetery in Galesburg certainly adds to the history lesson.

KNOXVILLE LOST SEAT

The tiny hamlet of Henderson, north of Galesburg, became the first unofficial seat of government for the current Knox County in the 1830s. When Knox County became incorporated, Knoxville was chosen as the official seat of government and a permanent courthouse was constructed on the public square in 1840. The stately, two-story, red and white brick structure is still in use today as a museum and meeting center.

Unfortunately, from the beginning, a fight ensued with Knoxville's neighbor Galesburg, located a mere five miles to the west. The ensuing tiff was over who should have the legal right to host the county seat. Speculation remains today that Galesburg's success in outdueling Knoxville for the railroad right of way enhanced the battle. A case can be built that the rapid growth of Galesburg encouraged a bullish right to take over the county seat of government.

It is interesting to note that William Selden Gale, son of Reverend George Washington Gale, who established Galesburg and Knox College,

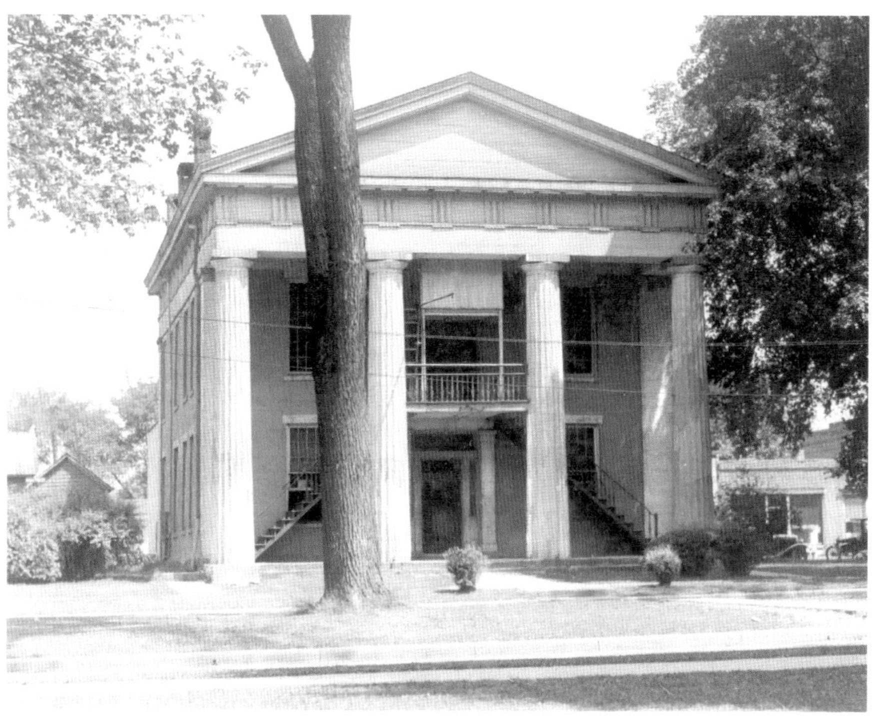

The original Knox County Courthouse in Knoxville, Illinois.

almost single-handedly took on the task of removing the county seat from Knoxville. With the coming of the railroad and the rapid burst of Galesburg's population, the need for attorneys to handle the surge of land property acquisitions soared. These same lawyers soon became extremely irked to drive the five miles from Galesburg to Knoxville to complete their legal matters. It seemed that the main topic became, "Let's move the county seat to Galesburg!"

Knoxville seemed to have the better right to retain the county seat. It was the geographic center of the county and was for sure more accessible to the other townships. The people of Knoxville had built a fine courthouse and its residents and the majority of the adjoining townships couldn't see any advantage in a change. Initially, the original sixteen townships, with little exception, were satisfied to retain Knoxville as their county seat.

Although the odds seemed to be stacked high against Galesburg obtaining rights to the county seat, young Selden Gale proved to be a tenacious fighter and political strategist. Gale was one of two representatives of

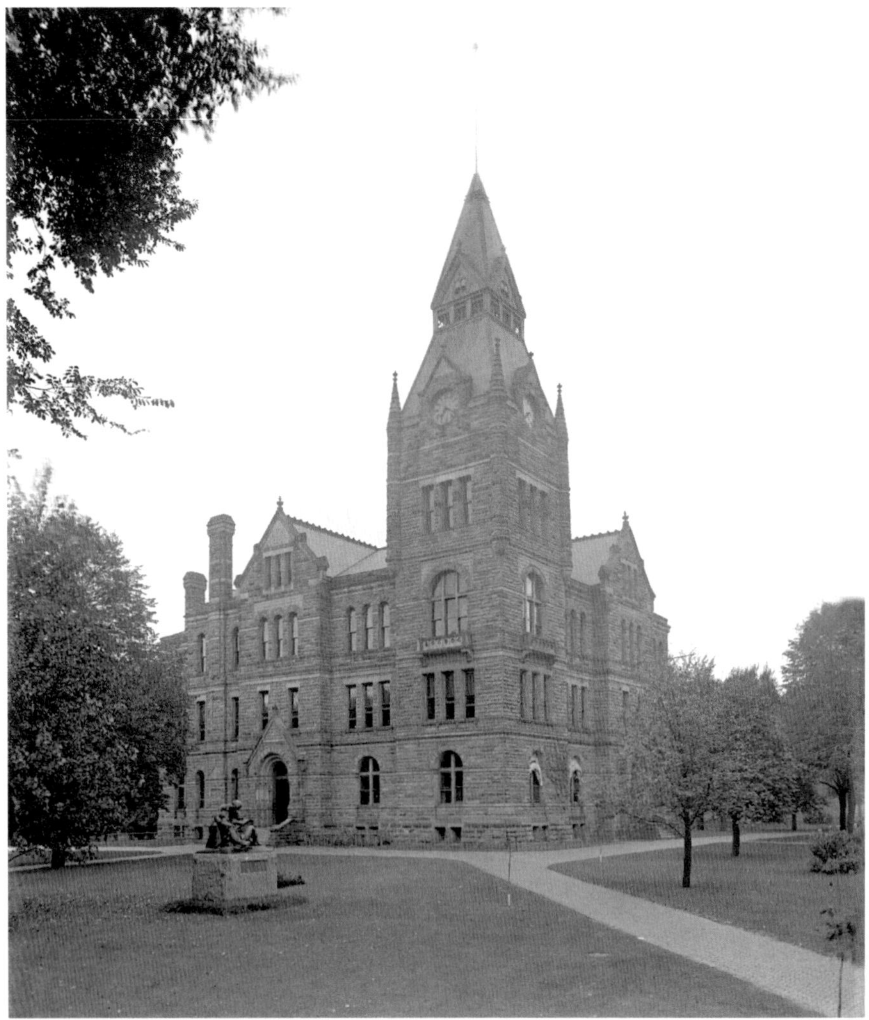

The current Knox County Courthouse in Galesburg, Illinois.

Galesburg on the county board of supervisors and quietly laid out his plans to eventually secure a majority on the side of Galesburg.

Meanwhile, down in Springfield, Galesburg had suddenly come into political favor in the state legislature. Prior to the Civil War, the state legislative body had been on unfriendly terms with abolitionist Galesburg and had sided with proslavery Knoxville during the railroad controversy. The tables became turned when both the governor and legislature became Republican like Galesburg. The powerful Galesburg lobby, led by Selden Gale, went into action and succeeded in pushing through legislation that allowed putting the issue of where the Knox County seat of government should be located before the county electorate.

Even though Galesburg's wishes were popular in Springfield, the feelings of the majority of Knox County residents changed very little. An election was held and Knoxville retained the county seat by a large majority vote. The *Galesburg Free Press* newspaper visibly mourned the defeat. Another man might have given up the fight; however, the defeat gave Selden Gale additional incentive. The continued fight to move the county seat raised a constant shadow over each ensuing meeting of the board of supervisors.

Eventually the persistence and political wrangling of Gale resulted in the supervisors becoming deadlocked on the issue, thirteen to thirteen. The normal proceedings of the supervisors became so tied up that the public business was interfered with. Balloting for a chairman lasted three days, and the bickering and squabbling between rival parties became so intense that the choosing of the chairman had to be decided by the flip of a coin.

Galesburg's next move was to successfully elect Selden Gale to the state legislature. As soon as Gale arrived in Springfield, he rounded up his forces and passed legislation to have another county vote to decide the long-standing issue. Election day came on April 6, 1869. When the vote was concluded, a multitude of citizens flocked to the smoky rooms of the courthouse to witness tellers count the returns. The tabulating went on throughout the night. Mysteriously enough, Knoxville did not show its hand until early the following day. To the surprise of hundreds, the final results revealed that Knoxville had once again prevailed by a majority of 247.

"Fraud!" screamed Galesburg. "You too!" answered Knoxville. The Galesburg people were greatly angered; Knoxville's vote was three times as large as its perceived population. The whole county was in uproar, and a special meeting of the supervisors and an eventual court battle revealed that Knoxville's legal vote total was 639, instead of 1,520. Later, it was revealed that residents of Knoxville truly thought that Galesburg would stuff the ballot boxes and Knoxville people decided to "out-stuff 'em."

To make a very long story short, Galesburg and Selden Gale succeeded in removing the county seat from Knoxville. One old-timer said, "There's nothing like a county seat fight to stir up the people inside, people go just plum crazy!"

Whether there are still people who are bitter about the unfortunate fight for the location of the seat of Knox County government is not completely clear. One might easily conclude that Knoxville should be saluted for losing the battle with "class" and, for sure, continues displaying that "class" to this day.

A GALESBURG CHRISTMAS GIFT

Once upon a time, specifically Christmas 1840, a new Galesburg family received a special gift.

To fully understand the significance of how special, we need to revisit Crottenneck, New York, during September 1840. Abram Danforth, a once thriving New York City merchant, until the crash of 1837, was invited to settle in the new Galesburg, Illinois, by early resident Levi Simmons. Although Abram, his wife and six children were very excited, they were most reluctant to leave Brother Josiah behind. Josiah, a bachelor, had taken in the Danforth family during hard times. The six Danforth children—four boys and two girls—were favorites of Josiah. Uncle Josiah never failed to make Christmas the best for the children.

Josiah reluctantly gave his blessings to the Danforth family to try the new surroundings in Galesburg. He did warn them that the country was very unsettled, had Indians prowling around at night and that they might not ever make it to their hoped-for destination. Josiah explained that Galesburg was founded by a man named Gale, who was a Christian philanthropist, and that a better man had never lived.

Uncle Josiah made sure that the family was well equipped and made them a present of $500. The Danforth family arrived safely in Galesburg on July 4, 1840. There were few houses and they were obliged to establish themselves in a deserted cabin in Henderson Grove. The land proved to be some of the most fertile in the country and plenty of water was at hand.

Unfortunately, Abram eventually became very homesick and wanted to go back to New York. The task of making a home became herculean. One of his horses died, the cost of lumber was very high and a cow had to be bought. His wife stated that she was going to stay and educate the six children. One of the incentives afforded the Danforths for settling in Galesburg was fifty years of educational scholarships.

December came and nothing directly was heard from Uncle Josiah, except through another friend that he was very sick. The children began to think about Christmas. The boys had begged Uncle Josiah to come out to Galesburg and be with them at Christmastime. "Trust me, I'll see to that," replied the good uncle. The entire family questioned if Josiah would keep his promise or possibly send gifts. As Christmas drew closer, the children feared their uncle may be dead and the tears flowed.

Mother Danforth quickly changed the subject and talked about their plum cake for Christmas—it would be cornbread with dried blackberries. Their father remained silent and feared for the worst.

The stagecoach brought mail from Peoria twice a week when it was able to get through. A family member faithfully met the stage each Tuesday and Friday in hopes that a package or Uncle Josiah would arrive. When the father attempted to meet the stagecoach on December 15, he was informed that the Spoon River had overflowed its banks and the stage could not cross.

Hopes rose a few days before Christmas when the postmaster rode horseback to the Danforth cabin to deliver a letter from Crottenneck, New York. The postmaster was not able to turn the letter over to the family, as they did not have the twenty-five cents' postage that was due. The family was devastated; how would they possibly raise the funds to acquire the letter? Mother Danforth announced that she had saved two dozen eggs for Christmas and would now sell them to obtain the letter. Sadly, the sale of eggs was not sufficient to fetch the letter.

The family became more despondent by the hour. The children pondered that Santa would never find their chimney.

While the children were parching corn and playing games on Christmas Day, the horn of the Peoria stage could be heard in the distance. Mr. Danforth claimed that the sounds of the stage were growing nearer by the second. Mrs. Danforth said it sounded like it was on the Knoxville Road. Finally, the stage stopped right in front of the Danforth front door and out jumped a jolly old man, who yelled "Merry Christmas!" to all.

Yes, the jolly old man was Uncle Josiah! He hugged and kissed them all and everyone cried with joy. The merry days lasted for what seemed an eternity. Uncle Josiah brought cheer, comfort and money to ensure a prosperous life in Galesburg.

Wishing all of you a visit from your Uncle Josiah during the holiday season and into the New Year.

Almost Became Galesburgh

Galesburg was named after one of its founders and nearby towns were named for a multitude of reasons. It was not uncommon for original town names to change from time to time. The idea of founding a colony

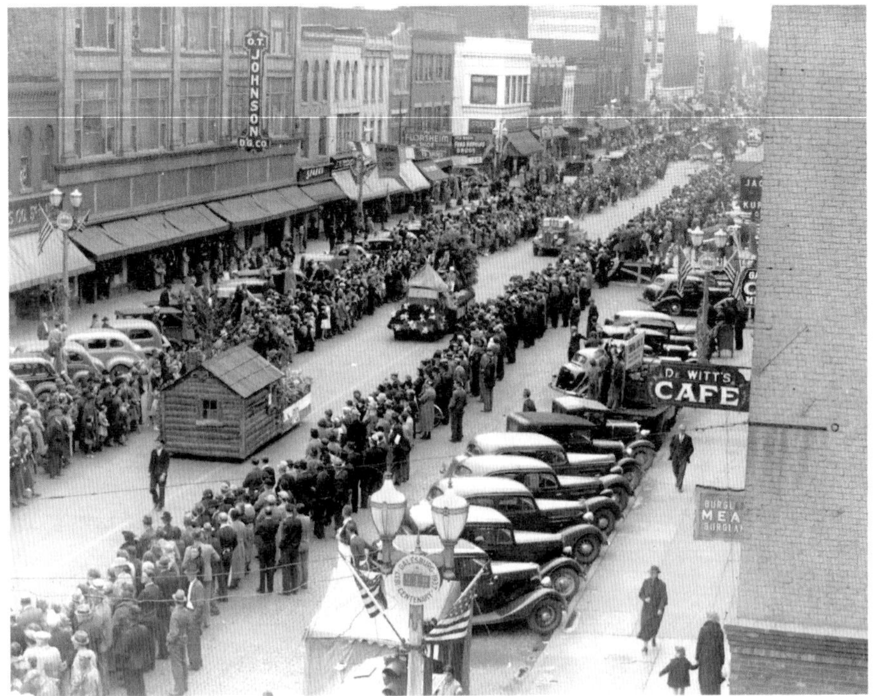

Galesburg centenary parade, 1937. The O.T. Johnson Big Store is in the background.

here originated with Reverend G.W. Gale in 1834. His goal and passion was to establish a colony to enhance the effort with a college. He shared his ideas with close friends in New York and they approved his plans in early 1835.

On May 6, 1835, a group of subscribers headed to Illinois and purchased seventeen acres of land for $1.25 per acre. On January 7, 1836, the group of subscribers met at Whitesboro, New York, projected the town to be Galesburg and proposed that the institution of higher learning would become Knox Manual Labor College. A plat of land was laid out consisting of approximately ten thousand acres at a cost of $16,559.70, which included exploring expenses. A town was laid out in the center of the plat to include divided acres for a school, cemetery, meetinghouse and parsonage. The remaining acres were divided into farms and appraised at the average price of $5.00 per acre.

An act to incorporate the city of Galesburg was approved by the state legislature on February 14, 1857, and the general charter was approved on April 10, 1872. The charter called for the election of a mayor, fourteen aldermen, a city treasurer, clerk and attorney. The initial controversy to face the early settlers was whether a license to sell liquor would be allowed.

Unlike many surrounding communities, the name Galesburg and its spelling were accepted and not tampered with until 1918. In July 1918, a group of patriotic residents began a campaign to change the spelling by adding an "h" to the end, making it "Galesburgh." Several businessmen endorsed the new spelling. They formed the Pro-Ally Galesburgh Committee and attempted to recruit public support.

An editorial comment on the subject appeared in the *Moline Daily Dispatch* newspaper. It read in part, "There is one time when a silent 'H' becomes more eloquent and that is when it spells the difference between a German and an Anglo-Saxon name." It further pointed out that the name Galesburg in its present form is distinctly German, but by simply adding the "h" it immediately becomes a good old Anglo-Saxon word. The *New York Times* jumped into the fray and disagreed with the Quad-City newspaper by proclaiming that "Burg" is English, not German.

Those proposing the spelling change apparently were reluctant to reveal their true motives, which probably varied. It is apparent that the proposal, no matter how valid or silly, died a slow death and the town is still spelled Galesburg.

Swedish Newspaper

January 3, 1955, was a red-letter day in the annals of the Augustana Lutheran Church, completing one hundred years since the first church newspaper was published. On January 3, 1855, Dr. T.N. Hasselquist, pastor of Galesburg's First Lutheran Church, published the first Swedish newspaper. It marked the centennial of the beginnings of our religious press.

The publication house was located at the southeastern corner of Seminary and North Streets. At the top of the front page of the semimonthly publication was the following heading:

HEMLANDET
Det Gamla och Det Nya
Vol. 1, Galesburg, Illinois
January 3, 1855, No. 1

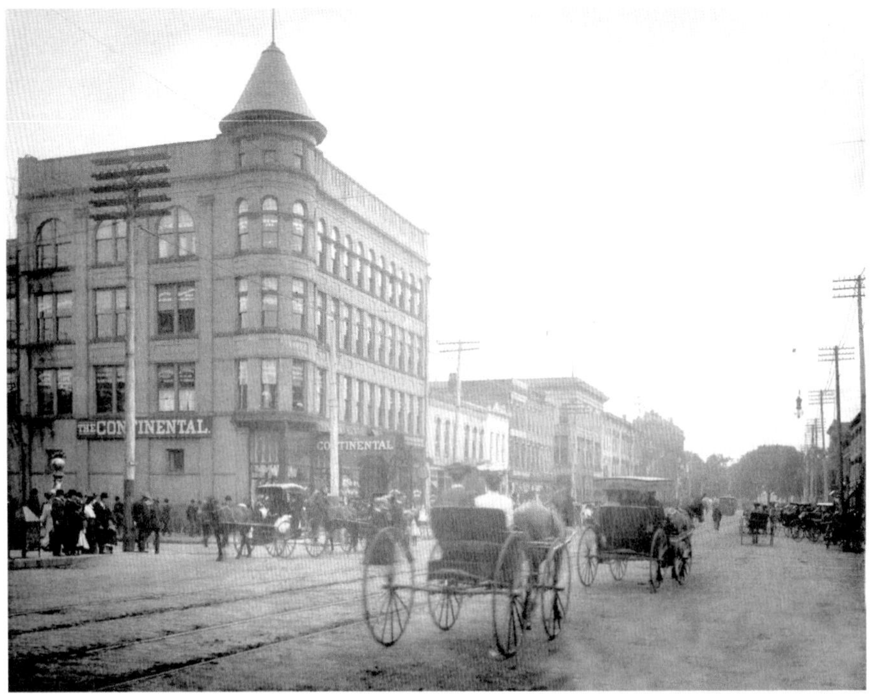

Galesburg downtown street scene, 1899. The surface is paved in brick with streetcar tracks in the middle.

Translated, the first line means "The Homeland." The second line means, "The Old and the New." The reference is to the two countries that were dear to the hearts of the early immigrants. These were "the Mother Country," the land of their birth, which they left behind, and "America," the new country, which they had learned to love and the land of their adoption.

Dr. Hasselquist announced that after five months of publication, the paper's circulation attained the six hundred mark. A printing press was obtained for $200. On March 1, 1855, German type equipment arrived in Galesburg from New York after part of the type in Roman characters had been set. The remainder of the paper was set in black letter type, which was generally used in Swedish print.

The Swedish newspaper contained two sections, one of religious and the other of secular news. Weekly publication was begun on May 1, 1856. Issues were captioned *Del Raetta Hemblandet* ("the *True Homeland*"), which stressed the "homeland above to which all believers look in faith." The name was changed to *Augustana* in 1868 and was combined with the *True Homeland* in 1869.

Trials of preparing the new publication were told by J. Oscar Backlund in his book, *A Century of the Swedish American Press*, published in 1952. Dr. Hasselquist obtained the services of a Swedish typesetter in Boston, Massachusetts, one N.P. Armstrong, native of Karlshamn, Sweden.

The final issue of the Galesburg Swedish newspaper was dated December 18, 1858, and had over one thousand subscribers.

CHAPTER 2

SUPER PERSON

Where Was Superman?

The Public Square in downtown Galesburg was known as Skid Row for a number of decades. Slowly, the multitude of taverns and flophouses disappeared from the landscape. A very successful urban renewal project in the mid-'60s resulted in the scene displayed today. Residents growing up in Galesburg during the '30s, '40s and '50s would undoubtedly be able to share interesting tales of happenings occurring on the Public Square. Retired Galesburg policemen would for sure have many horror stories to share. Galesburg firefighters also have memories of trips to the Public Square area.

Shortly before 7:30 a.m. on Sunday, November 5, 1958, all fire units were summoned to 5 Public Square. An out-of-control fire was spotted in the Peerless Market that resulted in over $30,000 damage to the structure, merchandise and fixtures. In addition, damage occurred to Barney's Lunchroom, located north of the burning three-story building.

The real highlight of the fire was the forced evacuation of Mrs. Helen Lescher Bessolo from an upstairs apartment above the grocery store. Mrs. Bessolo was rescued through an upper front window by firemen deploying the large hook and ladder fire truck. Fortunately, her seven pet dogs were saved by Barney McKay, whose restaurant adjoined the burning structure. Helen Bessolo was grateful for the help rendered by the firemen and Barney McKay; however, she would have preferred a rescue by her famous son. Helen was the mother of George Reeves, better known as Superman of radio, television and comic book fame. The episode prompted local residents and the media to ask, "Where Was Superman When His Mother Needed Him?"

HOLLYWOOD SUPER DEATH

The film *Hollywood Land* explores the mysterious death of George Reeves, who portrayed Superman during the 1950s. Reeves, whose mother Helen was from Galesburg, died from what authorities declared was a self-inflicted gunshot wound in his Beverly Hills, California home during the early hours of June 16, 1959.

Superman's mother, Helen Lescher Bessolo, was raised in Galesburg and owned several properties in her hometown at the time of her death in 1964. Mrs. Bessolo's father, George Lescher, founded the Lescher Drug Store at 15 East Main Street in downtown Galesburg that later became the historical Hawthorne Drug Store.

Many of Reeves's friends and fans, as well as his mother, disputed the suicide theory. His mother left Galesburg following her son's death and hired a private detective to investigate the tragedy. Reeves had signed a contract to perform an additional year of portraying Superman and was to marry Lenore Lemmon three days after his death. Another ironic twist was that he was scheduled to fight light-heavyweight boxing champion Archie Moore the day following his controversial death.

While living in Pasadena, Helen met and married Frank Bessolo, who would eventually adopt her young son George. Following George's graduation from a Pasadena Military School and three years of college, he served in the Army Air Corps during World War II for four years. His involvement with the Pasadena Playhouse resulted in a movie contract with Warner Bros.

Prior to his contract to portray Superman, George was cast as one of Vivien Leigh's suitors in the initial scene of *Gone with the Wind*. He also appeared with Claudette Colbert in *So Proudly We Hail* and numerous Hopalong Cassidy films.

George Reeves visited his mother in Galesburg several times during his adult life while portraying Superman. The late Stewart Hawthorne of Galesburg shared that George Reeves maintained an apartment above the current Turner Pharmacy on the Public Square when visiting his mother. Hawthorne also shared that he often visited with Superman Reeves as they sipped malted shakes at the Hawthorne Drug Store and played cards with Helen Bessolo.

Helen Lescher Bessolo passed away in Pasadena, California, on June 18, 1964, at the age of sixty-five. She had not returned to Galesburg since her son's death. Superman's mother willed her entire estate to her four surviving dogs. The estate of undetermined value, which included several Galesburg properties, was directed for the proper care, well-being and happiness of her beloved pets Little Helen, Paula, Bobbie and Poncho Bessolo. A Galesburg bank was named administrator.

In the movie *Hollywood Land*, George Reeves is played by actor Ben Affleck and Helen Bessolo is portrayed by actress Lois Smith.

It has been suggested that a sign be erected in the center park of the Public Square that reads, "Look Up at the Sky…It's a Bird…It's a Plane… No, It's Superman!"

Superman's Legacy Lives On

The movie *Hollywood Land* about George Reeves's death has raised more questions than answers and has produced additional information about his Galesburg connection. In the early morning hours of June 16, 1959, Helen Bessolo received a dreaded phone call in her Galesburg apartment informing her of the tragic death of her son George. Beverly Hills police concluded that Reeves had taken his own life.

Naturally, Helen Bessolo, being alone and not on good terms with her famous son, was very distraught. California authorities informed Helen that she would be responsible for making funeral arrangements. Helen was very reluctant to make the trip to California alone. Several days elapsed as Helen attempted to find a traveling companion. Fortunately, a Galesburg acquaintance, Mrs. Lyle Arie, agreed to accompany Helen Bessolo and one of her pet dogs on a train trip to California.

According to Lyle Arie, the local head of the Santa Fe Railroad provided a special train car for the trip. Lyle's husband Archie had helped construct the Galesburg Animal Shelter and Helen Bessolo had been a staunch supporter. Helen Bessolo would often visit the Arie home in Galesburg to watch the *Superman* episodes on television.

While in California, they stayed in a house owned by Helen Bessolo. Lyle Arie, at the request of Bessolo, went to the funeral home and made final arrangements for George Reeves's funeral and to ensure that he looked all right. Mrs. Arie stayed with Helen Bessolo for three weeks before returning to Galesburg. Lyle shared that the remainder of Helen's life was consumed trying to prove that her son's death was murder, not a suicide. She was not surprised that Helen Bessolo never returned to Galesburg before her death. Helen and Lyle corresponded by letter and phone often; however, they never were together again. Mrs. Arie still resides in Galesburg and is not surprised that the legacy of George Reeves continues fifty years after his death. Lyle believes that the truth behind Reeves's death will eventually be known, but maybe not in our lifetime.

Several local residents have come forward and shared their experiences with Helen Lescher Bessolo and her famous son. Former WGIL radio announcer Jim Dunlevey frequently received on-the-air calls from Helen Bessolo to report her taking in a stray dog. Jim said that her calls would always begin, "This is Mrs. Bessolo, Superman's mother."

Norma Lee Hroziencik of Galesburg shared her fleeting moment with the "Man of Steel." Norma Lee and her sister Gloria often visited their aunt, Marie Hickey, who lived in the Broadview Hotel on the Public Square during the 1950s. Aunt Marie was a close friend of Helen Bessolo, who would tell the sisters when her son would be visiting. Norma Lee and her sister were determined to meet Superman in person. One particular Saturday evening, the sisters walked along Main Street from the Public Square to the legendary O.T. Johnson Big Store in hopes of catching a glimpse of the famous actor. Suddenly, they spotted a well-dressed, handsome man, accompanied by a beautiful lady, departing the Big Store. Indeed, it was George Reeves of Superman fame. Reeves stopped and smiled at the sisters; however, during their excitement they failed to obtain an autograph. Speculation is that the lady with George Reeves was his wife, Ellanora Needles.

A multitude of questions remain about both the Galesburg connection to Superman and his mother Helen. The actual cause of Reeves's tragic death remains a controversy.

CHAPTER 3

VERSATILE POET

THE POET WAS A PLAYER

Galesburg lays claim to being the home of a famous poet, biographer and playwright named Carl. Now we will reveal the other side of the story.

Carl Sandburg, often called Charlie, dropped out of Galesburg's Douglas School at the conclusion of his eighth-grade studies. After working at a multitude of jobs, he was off to join the famous Sixth Illinois Infantry Volunteers doing battle in Puerto Rico.

At the age of eighteen, Charlie and his other Galesburg buddies were discharged from the successful war effort and returned home with about $100 each. Charlie gave $50 to his father and spent the remainder on a new bike, clothing and used schoolbooks as he prepared to enter Lombard College. Although he had dropped out of school in the eighth grade, the future poet was allowed to enter college as a special plan afforded to war veterans as part of the forerunner to the GI Bill of Rights. It was no secret that Charlie was facing a huge challenge. Six years away from the classroom, fighting on foreign soil and not looking forward to sitting through boring classroom lectures was going to make things difficult.

As a youngster, Charlie was fond of baseball; he was considered a walking encyclopedia on the sport and dreamed of playing in the big leagues. It was thought that the dream heavily outweighed the lad's actual ability. What happened shortly after Charlie enrolled at Lombard College would surprise even the most optimistic of local sports fans.

Many activities were available to Lombard students, including a full menu of sports. Another of Charlie's dreams was to play basketball, so when the coach announced tryouts, guess who walked on to show his skills? Sandburg not only made the team, but he also became a starting guard for the next four

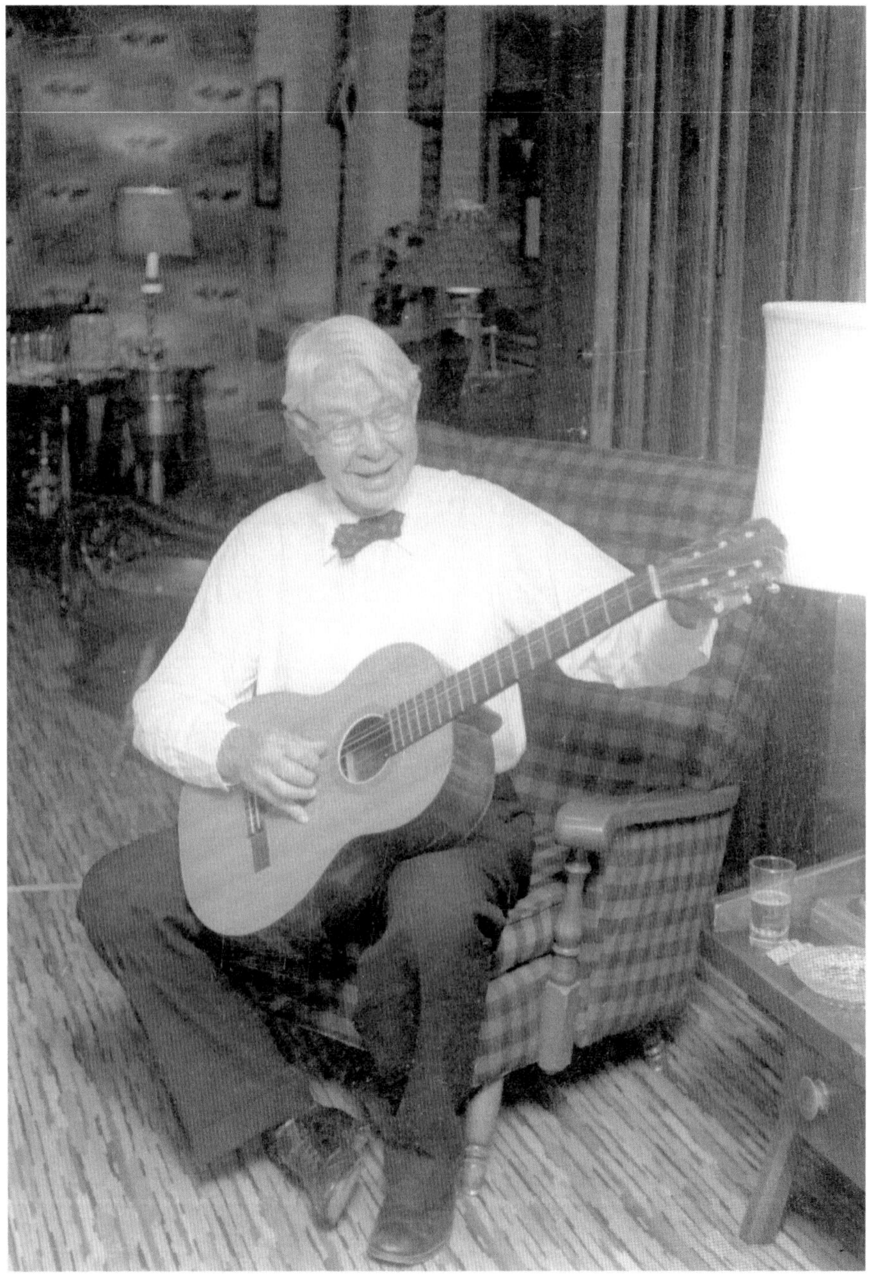

Galesburg poet Carl Sandburg playing guitar, 1958.

seasons. Basketball uniforms and game rules at that time were quite different from modern-day roundball. Charlie and his teammates wore tank tops and ankle-length tights with shorts over them. Also, the running shoes were quite different from the current expensive models. Although five personal fouls were allowed, upon the second infraction, the player was disqualified until the next basket was scored. When a ball went out of bounds, it was given to the first player touching it. If a team persisted in delaying tactics, the referee could call a foul.

Charlie's first collegiate game was against the local YMCA team, and the newspaper reports indicate that his superior defense aided in a Lombard victory. He took part in what would become classic matches between Lombard and crosstown rival Knox College. The second time the schools played, Charlie played a superior game and led his team to victory, sixteen to twelve. Bartlett of Lombard made the shot of the game by pitching the ball into the basket from the opposite side of the room. Exuberant Lombard supporters streamed out of the gym doors in prankish celebration and made life miserable for those living along East Knox, Pine, Whitesboro and Day Streets. The *Galesburg Daily* reported that several undergrads spent the night in the calaboose.

During Charlie's stellar Lombard basketball career, several exciting games were played against Monmouth College. In fact, on January 27, 1900, Charlie played in the first ever basketball game played by Monmouth College—Lombard won, eighteen to nine. During Charlie's four-year career at Lombard College, he played in games at over a dozen towns in Illinois, Iowa and Wisconsin.

Local sports scribes reported that Charlie Sandburg showed himself to be a very formidable player and competitor in basketball, football and baseball. His fellow teammates greatly benefited from his leadership. It should be noted that Charlie accomplished these feats while holding down a full-time job at the downtown fire station.

Yes, Charlie Sandburg, also known as Carl the poet, was also a very ordinary guy.

The Poet Played Basketball

On January 27, 1900, Monmouth College engaged in its first intercollegiate basketball game against Lombard College of Galesburg. Lombard defeated Monmouth by a score of eighteen to nine; however, that was not the total story of the inaugural game.

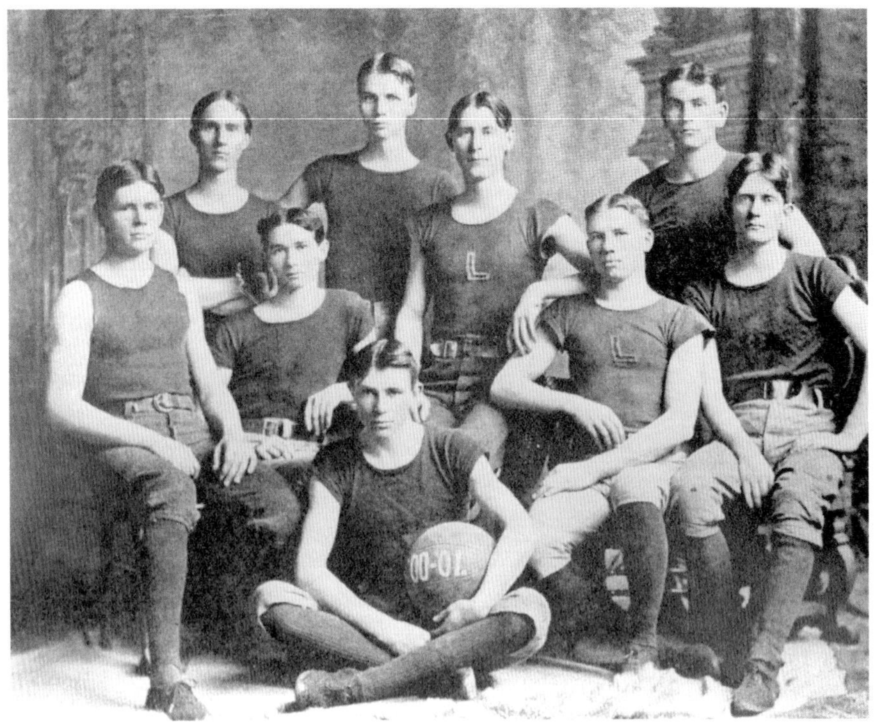

Lombard College basketball team, 1900. Poet Carl Sandburg is in front holding a basketball.

The game was played at the old Lombard Gym that no longer exists. Monmouth took an early three to two lead but quickly fell behind and could not keep up with the Lombard pace. The first half was twenty minutes long and for some unexplained reason the second half was only fifteen minutes in duration. The Galesburg newspaper reported that the Monmouth men were exhausted and discouraged. It was reported that if regulation time had been used in the second stanza, a much larger margin in the score would have resulted.

Playing for Monmouth College were McCoy, Gainer, Cusick, Clernand, Holmes, Firoved and Clarke. McCoy led Monmouth in scoring with three field goals. Lombard participants included Ericson, Bishop, Andrew, Brown, Fosher and Sandburg. Ericson led Lombard with three field goals.

Are you curious about the lad named Sandburg, who only scored one field goal for Lombard? The guard and captain of the Lombard team was none other than Carl August Sandburg. Young Carl became known worldwide as a famous poet and biographer. The Galesburg newspaper reported that one of the game's highlights occurred when Gainer and Sandburg performed an amusing impromptu acrobatic turn late in the game.

Later in the season, Carl Sandburg scored three goals in leading Lombard to a hard-fought fourteen to eleven victory over neighbor Knox College. It appeared to be the first ever game between the crosstown schools and was played in the Knox College Library Hall. An interesting aspect of the well-attended game was that play was delayed several times when the ball struck the glass chandelier above the center circle. Players of both teams were forced to sweep up broken glass in order to resume play.

Carl Was a Potter

Several column readers have indicated ownership of pottery items apparently made by Galesburg Pottery. Yes, Galesburg Pottery was in operation from 1891 until an unfortunate fire snuffed out the factory in 1897. It was located on South Pine Street between Lombard and Day Streets. To be even more specific, it was near the old narrow-gauge right of way, south of the Galesburg–Peoria Burlington Tracks. The father of Joliet prison warden Henry Hill served as the contractor who built the two-story brick structure in 1891. A man named Colwell, who came here from Pennsylvania, established the pottery.

Clay was shipped from Colchester, Illinois, via the Burlington Railroad on specially converted stock cars. Holes were cut in the tops of rail cars to help load the clay. The two large kilns that burned coal were too hot for local clay. Molds were made of plaster of Paris and the various jugs were turned out by hand.

Products produced at the pottery factory included crocks, jugs, jars, pie plates, piggy banks and various toy-type items. The items were shipped to all parts of the country. Salesmen J.P. Kidder and George Longbrake traveled by horse and wagon throughout northern Illinois to peddle the products. They would furnish their own food and stay nights in farm barns. It was reported that many interesting stories resulted from their jaunts.

A large pond was located adjacent to the factory to furnish water to mix the Colchester Clay. The pond was originally created to provide clay and dirt for landscaping the newly constructed Knox County Courthouse. Neighborhood children would often swim in the pond until Galesburg chief of police I.N. Coakley would scare them away.

Initially, the Galesburg Pottery Works employed 20 to 30 men and a few women. During peak operations in the mid-1890s, there were as many as

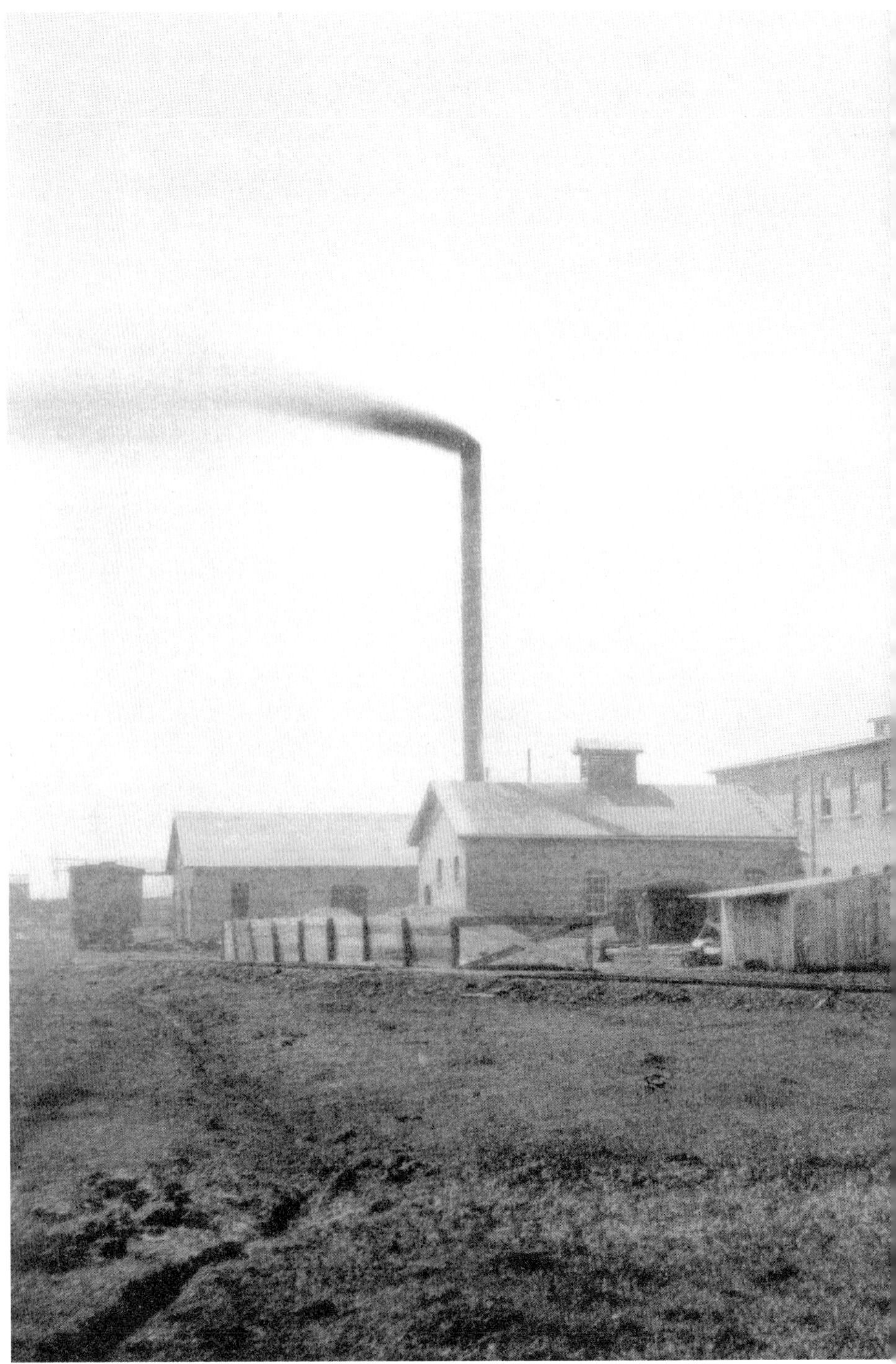

Galesburg Pottery Co., where poet Carl Sandburg was employed during his youth.

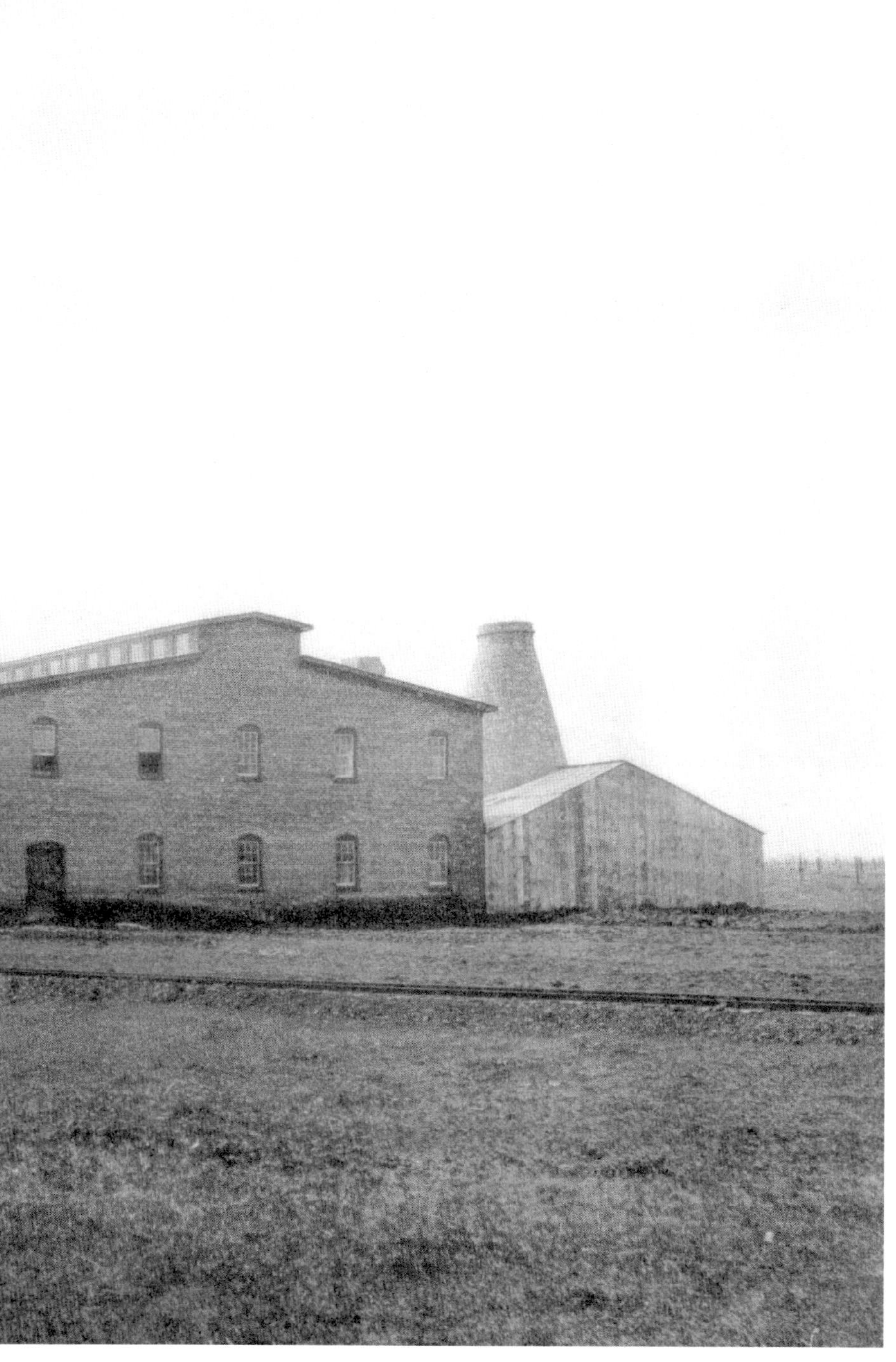

150 employees. Among those working at the pottery were Galesburg poet Carl Sandburg and Eddy (Frank Williams) Allen, who later starred as a member of the WLS Barn Dance Troupe. Many will probably remember other employees, including Charles House, Frank Patch, F.A. Harshbarger, Henry Gustafson, Clif Avery, George Anderson, Bessie Bloomberg, Ollie Harttrader, G.G. Heath, Bob McGuire, William Strandberg, John McQueeney, Fowler Vest, Joe Vest, Ed Beckman, Oscar Nelson, Ida Peterson, Cora Ford, Alfred Newberg and Charles Seeley. Local residents Adolph Weinberg and Alonzo Paden owned the Galesburg Pottery Factory when a disastrous fire leveled the facility on October 13, 1897.

Several months ago, column readers scurried to their medicine cabinets to check for Mother Berg's Salve. Today, they might check pieces of pottery for the inscription "Galesburg Pottery."

POET RECEIVES HIGH SCHOOL DIPLOMA

One of Galesburg's favorite sons, Carl August Sandburg, was born January 6, 1878, in a three-room cottage on East Third Street. You name it and Carl probably did it during his lifetime. He became world famous as a poet, biographer, journalist, novelist and folklorist. He described himself as a stranger, a seeker, a traveler, a singer and an eternal hobo.

One of the remarkable traits of Carl Sandburg was his varied accomplishments with only a scattered and often interrupted formal education. One of the little-known facts about Carl was that he actually spoke Swedish before he learned English. Charlie, as he was known, began his formal education in the first-grade classroom of Miss Flora Ward at the Seventh Ward School on Galesburg's Southside.

After successfully completing the fourth grade at the Seventh Ward School, Charlie Sandburg attended the fifth grade in downtown Galesburg at the Churchill Grammar School. Charlie completed the eighth grade at Churchill when he was fourteen years old and ended his schooling with a decision not to attend Galesburg High School. The main reason for his dropping out of school was to go into the workplace and help finance the further education of his sister Mary.

At the age of twenty, Charlie successfully fibbed about his age and was sworn into Company C, Sixth Infantry Regiment, Illinois Volunteers. Ten thousand Knox County residents assembled at the Chicago, Burlington and Quincy (CB&Q) Rail Station to send Sandburg and his colleagues off on a journey that would take them to an anticipated battle in Guantanamo Bay,

Cuba. In 1898, Private Charles August Sandburg and Company C were welcomed home to Galesburg as war heroes.

Following his discharge from the army and becoming a regular citizen, Charlie intended to set out and further explore the country with the hoboes. Although he had grown up in Galesburg roaming the lawns and buildings of both Lombard and Knox Colleges, he had no intentions, in his wildest dreams, of furthering his education. His life was to change forever when he discovered that he was afforded free tuition at Lombard College as a war veteran. He was accepted as a student at Lombard, although he had not attended high school.

Charlie Sandburg attended Lombard College for the next four years and became the most popular student on the Southside campus. He not only became an accomplished student, but he also excelled as an athlete. Sandburg captained the basketball team during his four years at the school. Midway through his time at Lombard College, Charlie was afforded an appointment by local Congressman George Prince to attend the United States Military Academy at West Point. Given little time to study for the entrance exam, he failed the difficult test and remained at Lombard College.

During the spring of his fourth year at Lombard, Carl August Sandburg abruptly decided to end his formal education for good without a degree. Thus, Sandburg headed for the big world beyond college days, with an eighth-grade education and what he considered four well-spent years at Lombard College.

Carl Sandburg often quipped that two of his most desired achievements would have been to become a Major League baseball player and to have graduated from his hometown high school. Charlie received a multitude of honorary degrees in his illustrious lifetime, including one from Knox College in 1928.

In May 1963, the District #205 School Board and the graduating class of Galesburg High School bestowed a high school diploma on Galesburg's favorite son. The 1963 senior class at Galesburg High voted to include Sandburg as a member of its graduating class.

Although Carl August Sandburg was a school dropout in his hometown, there is little doubt that no dropout ever became so famous.

CHAPTER 4

EXECUTIVE VISITS

Presidents Visit

Fifteen men who have served as president of the United States have visited Galesburg. In recent years, both former president William Jefferson Clinton and current president Barack Obama have presented the commencement address at Knox College. President Barack Obama gave the commencement address at Knox on June 4, 2005, and Clinton's presentation was on June 2, 2007. While the sitting president, Clinton also spoke at both Carl Sandburg Community College and Galesburg High School on September 10, 1995.

On October 7, 1858, future U.S. president Abraham Lincoln debated Stephen Douglas on the east lawn of Old Main on the Knox College Campus as part of the famous Lincoln-Douglas Debates. Lincoln's first excursion to Galesburg occurred on August 24, 1858, when he arrived on the Peoria & Oquawka Railroad. His short stopover before departing for Augusta, Illinois, included a visit to the Bancroft House Hotel located adjacent to the Knox College campus. Lincoln reportedly took time for a haircut in downtown Galesburg.

Of the fifteen men who visited Galesburg and served as U.S. presidents, five—Rutherford Hayes, Benjamin Harrison, William McKinley, Harry Truman and Bill Clinton—were actually the chief executive while here. George H.W. Bush spoke on the Knox Campus while vice president of the United States. U.S. Grant and Teddy Roosevelt were in Galesburg both before and after their presidencies. William Taft, Franklin Roosevelt, Ronald Reagan, Gerald Ford and George H.W. Bush visited Galesburg prior to becoming president. Dwight "Ike" Eisenhower's journey to Galesburg occurred following his presidency.

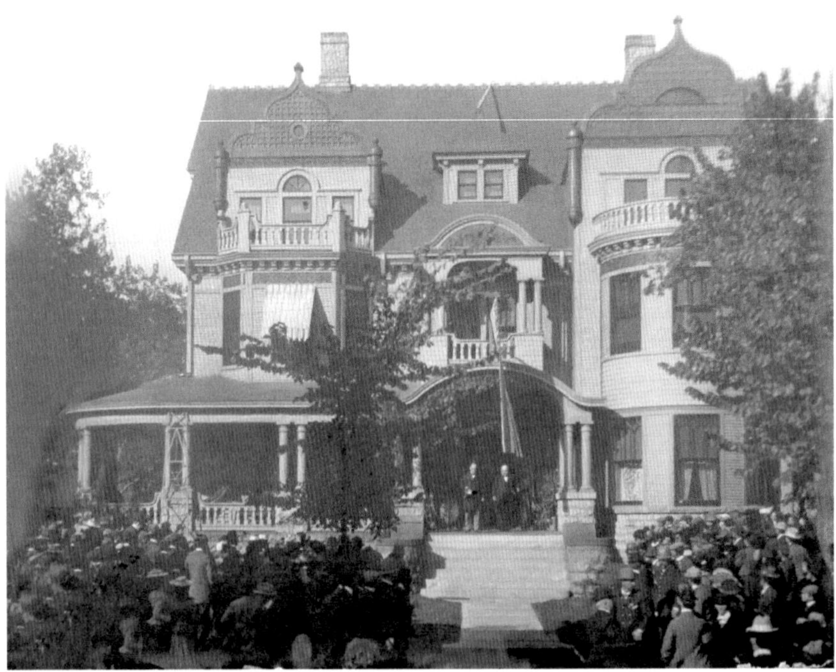

President William McKinley on the porch of the Clark E. Carr home in 1899. A presidential cabinet meeting was held during his visit to the Carr home.

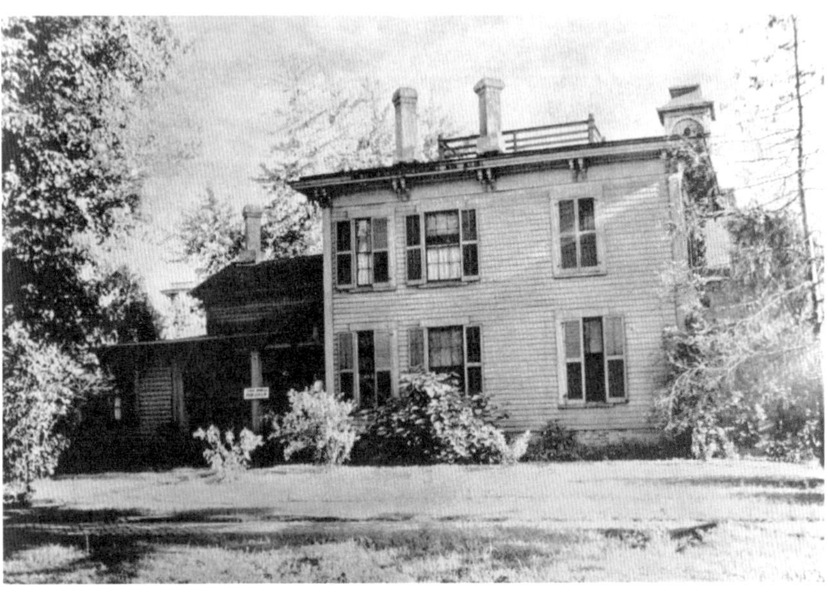

The home of Galesburg mayor Sanderson, where Abe Lincoln stayed overnight following his famous debate with Stephen Douglas on October 7, 1858.

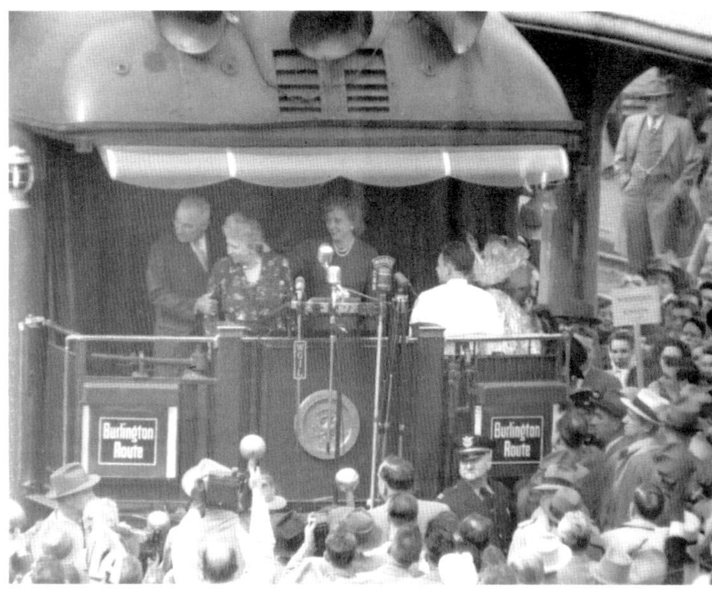

President Harry Truman on the back of the campaign train in Galesburg, 1950. Truman's wife Bess and daughter Margaret are also pictured.

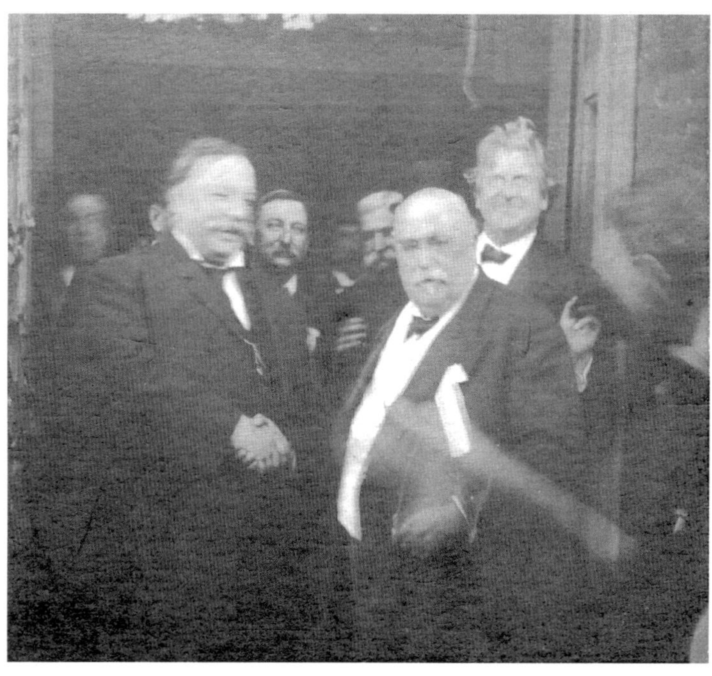

President Taft at Knox College, 1908. He is shown with Clark E. Carr at the site of the famous Lincoln-Douglas Debate.

The first sitting U.S. president to visit Galesburg was Rutherford B. Hayes on September 23, 1879. Hayes, accompanied by his wife Lucy and Generals Sherman and Sheridan, appeared during a twenty-one-minute stopover at the depot grounds near the Knox College Campus. Hayes gave a brief speech before five thousand curious onlookers.

On October 8, 1890, the twenty-third U.S. president, Benjamin Harrison, was greeted at the "Q" Railroad Depot on North Seminary Street by over ten thousand well-wishers. A gala parade of thousands took place as downtown Main Street was decorated from the Public Square to Seminary Street for the occasion. President Harrison took part in the laying of the cornerstone for the Alumni Hall on the Knox College Campus. President Harrison and his entourage dined at the Union Hotel during the noon hour and took part in a grand banquet at the Odd Fellow Hall at Main and Seminary Streets during the evening.

One of the most elaborate visits occurred during October 1899, when U.S. president William McKinley, his wife Ida and his entire cabinet came to Galesburg for the second celebration of the Lincoln-Douglas Debates. President McKinley and his wife, along with his private secretary George Coutelyou, stayed at the Clark E. Carr residence on North Prairie Street. Legend has it that the first ever full cabinet meeting outside of the nation's capital was held at the Carr residence.

Thousands of area residents greeted President Harry Truman, his wife Bess and daughter Margaret from the rear platform of a CB&Q train on May 8, 1950, at the depot on North Seminary Street. President Truman was presented a huge birthday cake by Mayor Ralph Johnson and a box of divinity candy by his cousin, Ruth Peterson, who resided on Arnold Street in Galesburg.

Ronald Reagan, the fortieth president of the United States, spoke during the annual Knox County Republicans' Lincoln Day Dinner at Knox College on March 16, 1980. The occasion was Reagan's first visit back to Galesburg since 1917, when he lived on North Kellogg Street and attended both first and second grades at Silas Willard School. Vice President George H.W. Bush spoke at the Lincoln Day Dinner at Knox College on March 13, 1988.

Gerald Ford, who served as the thirty-eighth president of the United States, spoke at a Knox County Republican fundraiser on July 29, 1966. The five-dollar-per-plate picnic was held near the bandstand at Galesburg's Lincoln Park. Ford, at the time, was minority leader of the U.S. House of Representatives.

Visits to Galesburg
of Those Serving as President of the United States

Abraham Lincoln	August 24, 1858	October 7, 1858
Ulysses Grant	1868	October 27, 1879
Rutherford Hayes	September 23, 1879	
Benjamin Harrison	October 8, 1890	
William McKinley	October 6–7, 1899	
Theodore Roosevelt	July 5, 1900	April 16, 1912
William Howard Taft	October 7, 1908	
Franklin Roosevelt	October 1, 1920	
Harry Truman	May 8, 1950	
Gerald Ford	July 29, 1966	
Dwight Eisenhower	May 1967	
Ronald Reagan	March 16, 1980	
George H.W. Bush	March 13, 1988	
William Clinton	September 10, 1995	June 2, 2007
Barack Obama	June 4, 2005	several other visits

Ron Goes to School

Jack and Nelle Reagan packed their belongings and rode the train to Galesburg in December 1915. The Reagans, along with sons Neil and Ronald, were very pleased to leave the crowded conditions of Chicago. A relative of Jack Reagan provided a job of selling shoes at the Big Store in downtown Galesburg.

Neil Reagan, then age seven, immediately enrolled at Silas Willard School on East Fremont Street less than two blocks from home. Due to the fact that Galesburg didn't provide kindergarten, Nelle Reagan home-schooled young Ronald and taught him to read.

Since Ronald Reagan was born in February, he didn't enter Silas Willard School until he was seven years old. The future U.S. president quickly became a star pupil in Mrs. Alice Colville's first-grade room. A March 1918 report card reveals near perfect marks in all subjects.

Reagan's first-grade classroom included fifteen students—six girls and nine boys. Ron's fellow classmates included Donald Bocox, Clarence Booth, Duane Dailey, Doris Dunbar, Iasbel Holmes, Henry Inness, Ralph Johnson, Stephen Junk, Pauline Lindquist, Eleanor Lundeen, Elizabeth Oberg, Baxter Reid, Leonard Sauter and Hazel Wallace. Only a couple of the classmates have been identified; it is not known if any are still living.

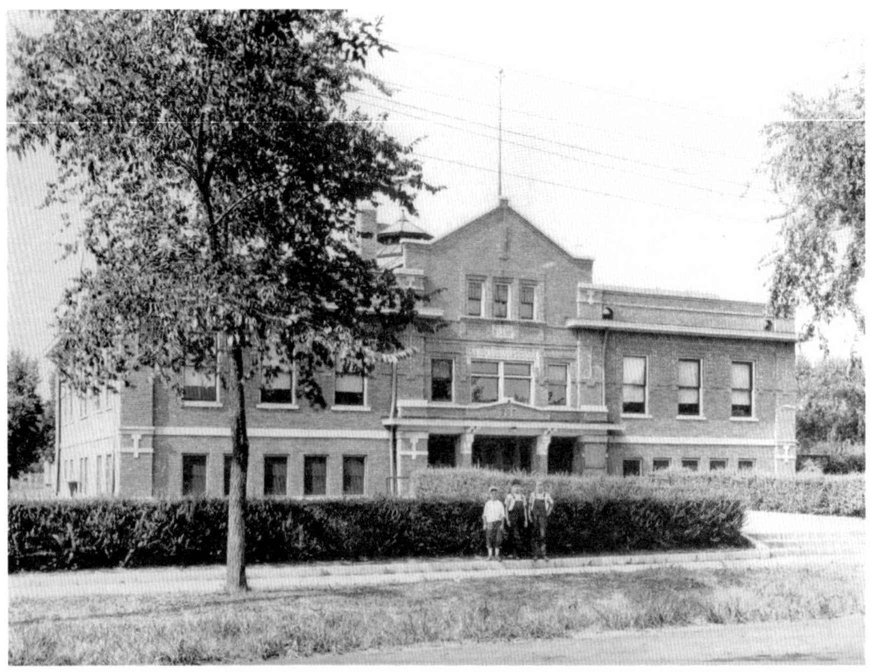

Silas Willard School in Galesburg, where former president Ronald Reagan attended first grade.

Although Kellogg Street, where Reagan lived, was laid with brick, Fremont Street in front of Silas Willard School was of a dirt surface and would not be paved for over a dozen years. As noted in older photos, the school building was only a small portion of today's structure. Reagan's first-grade classroom is still intact, along with the cloakroom where Ronald hung his hat and coat during inclement weather.

Reagan fondly remembers his mother Nelle coordinating a big show at the school to raise money for the war effort. Father Jack shocked Nelle by coming onstage as a snake charmer, wearing a wig and a hula skirt. The area where school entertainment was usually provided is now a storage area next to the current music room.

Ron also attended second grade at Silas Willard before his family eventually moved to neighboring Monmouth at midterm.

Mike Kirk, a student at Silas Willard School in 1976, wrote a letter to California governor Ronald Reagan inviting him to an ice cream social at the school. Reagan sent his regrets and enclosed a check for ten dollars. When Mike realized that Reagan was running for president, he sent another letter requesting an autographed photo. Reagan surprised Mike and his

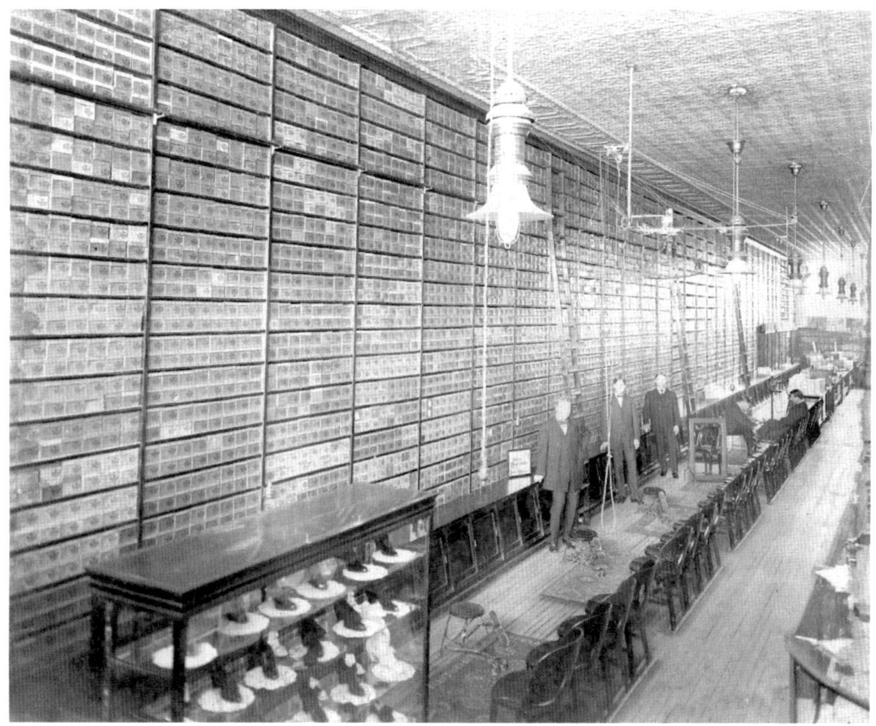

The shoe department of O.T. Johnson Big Store, where President Ronald Reagan's father was employed.

family by stopping off at their Brown Avenue residence to drop off a picture and jelly beans during a 1980 speech for the local Republican Party.

During May 1981, District #205 school board members, teachers and local businesses successfully raised funds to dedicate a commemorative plaque at the inside entrance to remind future students of Silas Willard that the fortieth president of the United States began his formal education at the school.

Ike Visits Galesburg

Fifteen men who served as president of the United States have visited Galesburg. Several vice presidents and those who ran unsuccessfully for the nation's top office have stopped by for various reasons. Abe Lincoln may be the most notable, with his involvement in the famous debate at Knox College in 1858.

No doubt the most unusual and least publicized visit by a chief executive occurred in May 1967. Dwight "Ike" Eisenhower and his wife Mamie arrived in Galesburg aboard the Santa Fe Chief. President Eisenhower persuaded train officials to make an unscheduled ten-minute layover at the depot. The occasion allowed the Eisenhowers to meet the Donald Marshall family of rural Knoxville. The Marshall family included father Donald, wife Beverly, daughters Sally, Donna and Michelle and son Mark. Along with the family was a black-and-white, eight-week-old Scottish border collie by the name of Ike.

Don Marshall's father, Harold, had become friends with Eisenhower in 1954 and presented Ike with a male border collie for his Gettysburg farm. Harold Marshall of Deer Creek, near Peoria, imported the Scotties from Scotland and sold the registered pups throughout the country. When Harold passed away in the spring of 1967, his son's family inherited the dogs.

Sally, then a sophomore at Knoxville High School, was told by her grandfather that Eisenhower wanted a female Scottie from the same bloodline. Thus, Sally took special care in picking out the special pup that eventually would be shipped to the Gettysburg farm.

The Eisenhowers and the entire Marshall family were thrilled for the opportunity to have pup Ike meet his future master. The Eisenhowers rode in a special car at the rear of the Sante Fe Chief, accompanied by a large contingent of Secret Service agents.

Mr. Beaumont, local station agent for the Santa Fe, also was responsible for the special stop and seemed as thrilled as anyone. The former president had been in ill health lately; however, he appeared to be in very good spirits and on the road to recovery.

Sally carried young Ike onto the train for inspection of Ike and Mamie. Eisenhower graciously posed for pictures with the entire family and seemed reluctant to leave the dog behind. When young Ike was ready to be shipped to Gettysburg, Knoxville vet Dr. Hoyme donated the necessary shots.

Border collies are excellent sheep and cattle dogs and make very gentle pets. These collies were sold regularly from the Marshall farm and shipped throughout the Midwest. The Marshall family eventually moved to the Roseville area and continued to raise the special collies. Sally, appropriately, became a nurse and the other children now live throughout the county like their famous Scottish border collies.

President's Mother Schooled in Knoxville

Knoxville, the oldest city in Knox County and originally the county seat, is celebrating its 175th birthday. Once the home of two colleges and the historic PEO Home and the site of the county fair for over 150 years, Knoxville was once the temporary home of a U.S. president's mother.

Dorothy Ayer Gardner, the mother of President Gerald R. Ford, attended St. Mary's College in Knoxville during 1911–12. Gardner graduated from high school in her hometown of Harvard in 1910 and enrolled in what was described as a "fashionable small college in Knoxville, Illinois." The picturesque all women's school was located on the northern edge of Knoxville. Originally the state-supported institution opened its doors in 1859 as Ewing Female University and ceased operation eight years later. In 1868, the Episcopal Diocese of Illinois accepted an offer from the State of Illinois to take over the elaborate three-story brick building with the promise to maintain a college for a minimum of four years.

Knox College graduate Dr. Charles Leffingwell became the first rector and founder. He described St. Mary's as "a school for young women who desire to continue their work two or three years beyond the course of the high school. A school home where girls would become better daughters; where they would be systematically trained for the duties of wifehood and motherhood; where they were encouraged to recognize, and where they were required to prepare for, their present and future obligations."

In the early years, the majority of students were from the Chicago area; however, nearly every state and many foreign countries were represented. Board and tuition was $600 yearly and included use of the gymnasium, recreation hall, bowling alley, swimming pool, library and all laboratories. Daughters of the clergy received $300 off their tuition.

Five elected representatives of the Episcopal Church Diocese of Chicago, Quincy and Springfield decreed school policy. Trustees representing the city of Knoxville included Harvey J. Butt, Dr. Louis Becker, John H. Lewis, Harley J. Charles and John Z. Carns. Many prominent persons throughout the country donated funds, including Illinois governors Clark E. Carr and G.A. Purington of Galesburg and Mamie Eisenhower.

Dorothy Gardner, mother of future president Gerald Ford, roomed with Marietta Hughes King of Omaha, Nebraska, during her schooling at St. Mary's. Marietta introduced her brother Leslie to Dorothy and the couple was married shortly after graduation in the summer of 1912. Dorothy and Leslie King gave birth to Leslie Jr. in July 1914. Unfortunately, Leslie King abused Dorothy on many occasions, prompting the young

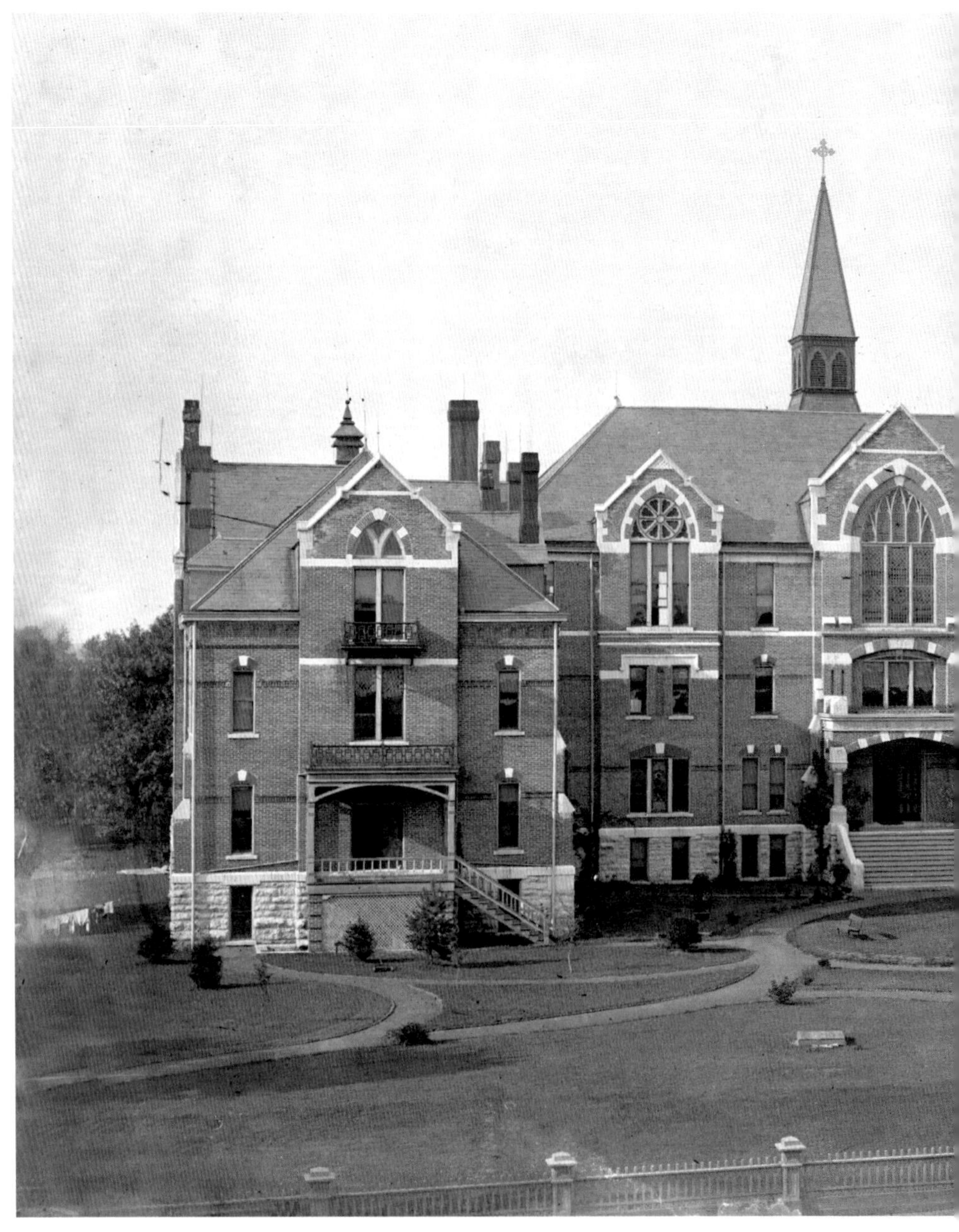

St. Mary's female school in Knoxville, Illinois, where President Gerald Ford's mother attended.

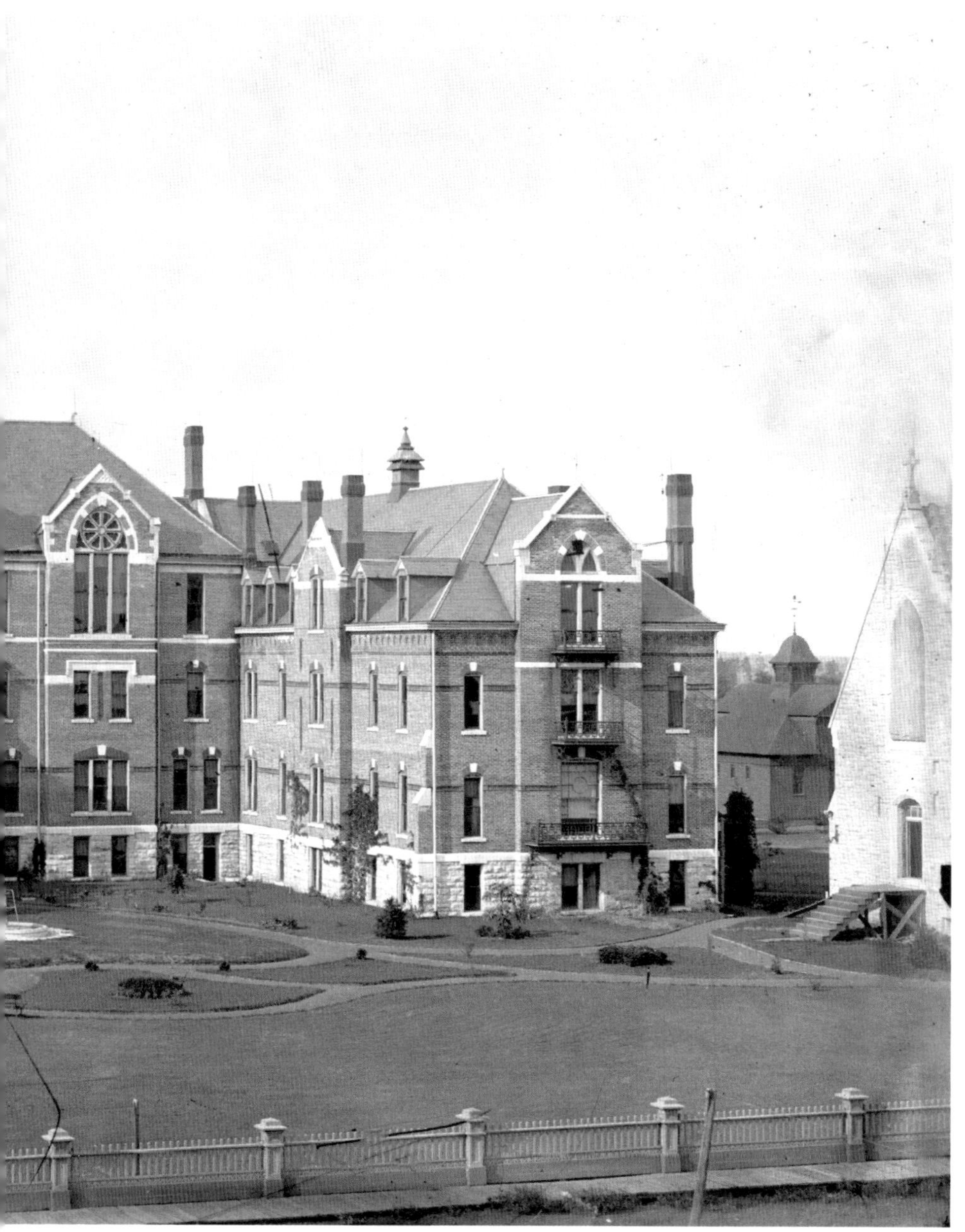

mother to flee to her parents' home when Leslie Jr. was only sixteen days old.

Dorothy King divorced the future president's father in December 1913. Three years later, Dorothy met Gerald R. Ford, a Grand Rapids businessman, and they were married in February 1917. Ford adopted four-year-old Leslie, who eventually changed his name to Gerald R. Ford Jr. The future president of the United States was not aware of the existence of his biological father until 1926, when he was thirteen years old.

Gerald Ford's mother graduated from St. Mary's School in Knoxville during June 1912 with a degree in domestic science. Dorothy was president of her graduating class and St. Elizabeth's Guild.

Dorothy Gardner Ford died in 1967 and is buried in the Woodlawn Cemetery in Grand Rapids beside her second husband, Gerald Ford. Her son, Gerald R. Ford Jr., served as president of the United States from 1974 to 1977.

With the exception of the beautiful chapel and the observatory, St. Mary's School in Knoxville is only a memory.

Ever wonder, would Gerald R. Ford Jr. have become the thirty-eighth president of the United States if not for St. Mary's School in Knoxville?

GOVERNOR FROM ONEIDA

Don Samuelson was born on July 27, 1913, at the farmstead home of his grandfather near Woodhull. The two-story farmhouse was heated with a big wood stove in the middle of the living room, had no electricity and the only available water was from a cistern in the backyard. The backyard also contained a "twin hole" comfort station. The family did have the luxury of a party line phone that was shared with fifteen other residences.

The one-room New Pine School that contained eight grades was Don's first real educational experience. He either walked across farm fields or rode his Shetland pony the one mile to school daily. Don transferred to the Woodhull Elementary School at the beginning of the fourth grade.

Just about the time Don had entered high school at Woodhull, the family moved to Ontario, halfway between Woodhull and Galesburg. Thus, young Don was required to enroll at Oneida High School starting his sophomore year. Oneida was cut in half by the CB&Q railroad tracks. The Knox County town actually had two separate and nearly equal business districts. Each side had its own restaurants, grocery and drugstore. In 1930, Oneida's population was six hundred.

Don adjusted to his new surroundings quickly and became active in school plays and athletics at Oneida High School. At six feet tall, Don became the center and leading scorer on the basketball team. At that time, Oneida played its home games in an old church where the sidelines were less than a foot from the wall. Don was the catcher on the softball team. Oneida did not have enough boys to field a football team.

No doubt track was his favorite sport, where he excelled in several events. During his senior year in 1932, Don won the Galesburg District Track championship in both the discus and shot put. Unfortunately, Oneida had only $4.65 in the sports treasury and informed Don that it would be unable to send him to the state meet in Champaign. Don was determined to participate in the state track finals since it was his senior year at Oneida High. He hitchhiked the 165 miles to Champaign-Urbana, stayed at the Tau Kappa Epsilon fraternity house and threw the discus and shot put.

Don received a scholarship to Knox College; however, his stay was short. He was seriously injured in a freshman football practice session and was forced to drop out of school. While visiting relatives in Florida in the mid-'30s, Don met Ruby Mayo and fell in love. The couple married in February 1936.

In 1940, Don joined the Davenport, Iowa fire department, and shortly thereafter, Ruby gave birth to their daughter Donna. Don became increasingly concerned about the United States' efforts during World War II, and one year after the Japanese bombing of Pearl Harbor he enlisted in the navy. During his enlistment he was stationed at the Farragut Naval Training Station in Idaho.

Don's time in Idaho turned out to be more than fate; it would eventually result in the most pivotal time period in his life. A case can be built that if Don had not enlisted in the navy he probably would not have retired from the fire department in Davenport.

Ruby, Don and their daughter Donna eventually made their home in Idaho. In 1960, Don was elected a state senator from Idaho. The family opened a sporting goods and gunsmith shop in Sandpoint and Don enjoyed his passion for hunting and fishing.

In 1966, while still serving in the Idaho senate, Don unsuccessfully tried to persuade a friend, former astronaut Alan Shepard, to run for Idaho governor. Instead, Don ended up informing Ruby and Donna that he would be running for governor. Don revealed in a book he penned, titled *His Hand on My Shoulder*, that after Ruby came off the ceiling three days later, she hesitantly agreed to join the campaign.

In January 1967, the 1932 graduate of Oneida High School, Donald William Samuelson, was inaugurated the twenty-fifth governor of the state of Idaho.

Don Samuelson died January 20, 2000, in his adopted and beloved Idaho. His daughter Donna lives in Sagle, Idaho, and I am indebted to her for her help with this wonderful story.

ARE YOU RELATED TO A GALESBURG MAYOR?

On August 29, 2008, John McCain, the Republican candidate for president, introduced the governor of Alaska, Sarah Palin, as his running mate. The surprise announcement sent media types scrambling to learn more details of Sarah Palin's life. Genealogists scurried to obtain information about her family tree. The search quickly revealed that the Republican's vice presidential "wannabe" had numerous traces in her family tree to Knox County.

Sarah Palin, the Republican Party's first female to be nominated for vice president, was born in Sandpoint, Idaho, on February 11, 1964, to Chuck and Sally Heath. The main bloodline relationship to Knox County and specifically Galesburg is through the Heath family connection. The Alaskan governor also has kinship ties to some of Galesburg's earliest families, namely Field and DeLong.

The most interesting kinship tie to Galesburg is by result of a marriage. In May 1837, Luman and Abigail (DeLong) Field left New York and settled in what is now Knoxville. Initially, Luman Field was a schoolteacher, but he later devoted his career to farming. This particular Field family had two children, a daughter Lucinda and a son Loyal Case.

During July 1837, William M. Heath came to Knoxville from New York. Shortly thereafter, Heath fell in love with Lucinda Field. On August 3, 1837, the couple became the first ever to be married in Knoxville. The Heaths raised eight children while farming in both rural Knoxville and Wataga. When William Heath died in 1882, Lucinda moved to Galesburg, where she passed away in 1899.

Lucinda's brother, Loyal Case Field, grew up on his parents' rural Knoxville farm, and his early educational experiences were limited. While in school he demonstrated a flair for artistic taste, revealing a fondness for drawing pictures of animals and natural scenery. Following school, he spent four years as a clerk in the Joseph Gay dry goods store in Knoxville. Following his father's death in 1846, he took care of the family farm. He then sold the farm, moved to Galesburg and bought a tin and hardware store. In 1848, Loyal married Clara Davison and she bore him five children.

Loyal Case Field then became a leading member of one of Galesburg's leading industries, Frost Manufacturing Company. Under his advice and management, the firm prospered and gained a wide reputation. Due to his abilities and integrity, his fellow citizens called upon him to enter local politics. Loyal Case served as a member of the Galesburg City Council in 1860, 1861, 1865 and 1866.

In 1872, an advertisement appeared in the *Galesburg Republican Register* newspaper containing names of over two hundred citizens requesting permission to place Loyal Case Field on the ballot for the position of mayor of Galesburg. Loyal consented to seek the mayoral post, and with the endorsement of the local newspaper he defeated the incumbent mayor, Timothy Nash, by a margin of 961 to 502. It is interesting to note that during that time, the position of mayor was only for a one-year term. Loyal Case passed away on July 11, 1899.

To make a long and very complicated story short, Sarah Palin's great-great-great-great-grandparents (by marriage) were the parents of Galesburg's twelfth mayor. This would make the 2008 Republican candidate for vice president the great-great-great-grandniece of the former Galesburg mayor.

Twelve family members, including the former Galesburg mayor and four members of the Heath family, are buried in Hope Cemetery.

Ironically, genealogists are now reporting that Sarah Palin is the eighth cousin of George W. Bush, the tenth cousin of Barack Obama and the twelfth cousin of John McCain.

Are we all related to each other?

CHAPTER 5

A SPORTING THING

Native Sons Make Big Show

Have you heard of "Old Hoss" or "Peaches" or "The Kid" or "Polly"? What they have in common is their ability to make the big time in Major League baseball. In fact, they were among ten men born in this area who played in the big leagues.

The first player born in Galesburg to play in the Major Leagues was Art "Old Hoss" Twineham. Art was born in Galesburg during 1866 and made his sporting debut on September 11, 1893, as a catcher for the St. Louis Browns, then a member of the National League. Twineham appeared in fifty-two games over two seasons, collecting fifty-two hits, hitting one homer, driving in seventeen runs and stealing two bases.

Knoxville lays claim to Roy Chamberlain "Polly" Wolfe, who was born in K-Ville during 1988. Wolfe broke into the Majors on September 22, 1912, as an outfielder with the Chicago White Sox. Roy appeared in nine games during two seasons, collecting six hits and stealing one base.

Karl Edward Swanson was born in North Henderson during 1900, and when he passed away on April 3, 2002, at the age of 101, he was the oldest living former Major Leaguer. Karl made his debut on August 12, 1928, as a second sacker for the Chicago White Sox. Swanson played in twenty-four games over two seasons, hitting safely nine times, driving in six runs and stealing three bases.

Oneida's native son, Ernest Follette "Kid" Mohler, was born in the northern Knox County community during 1874. Mohler made his Major League debut on September 29, 1894, as a second baseman for the Chicago White Sox. "Kid" Mohler appeared in only three games, collecting only one hit.

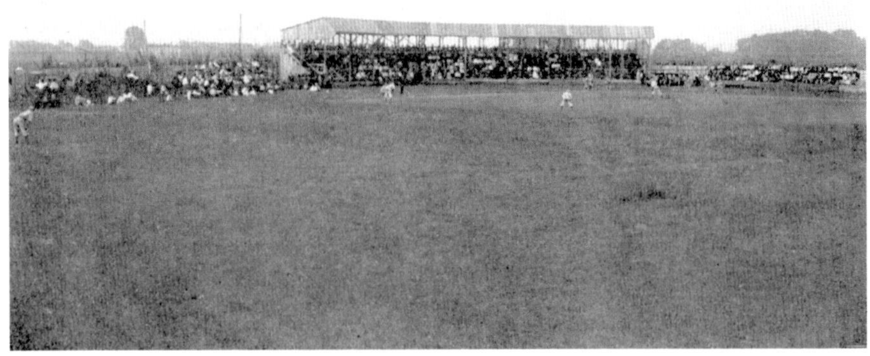

Illinois Baseball Park in Galesburg, 1909. Hall of Fame pitcher Grover Cleveland Alexander pitched his first professional game in this ballpark.

Aledo produced two players who reached the big show. Dewey McDougal appeared in twenty-one games with the St. Louis Browns in 1895 and 1896, winning 3 games as a pitcher and proving to be a decent hitter as he stroked six hits and drove in six runs. George Frederick "Peaches" Graham first appeared in the Majors with the Cleveland Indians during the 1902 season. Graham played over seven seasons and proved to be very versatile as a pitcher; he also played all other positions. He played in 373 games, mostly as a catcher. Graham's son Jack also played in the Majors and was third in the American League in homers during the 1949 season.

James "Hi" West was born in Roseville during 1884, attended Knox College and pitched for the Cleveland Indians during two seasons. West won five games and collected 4 hits. Bushnell's claim to fame was Earl Homer "Whitey" Sheely, who broke into the Majors with the White Sox as a first baseman in 1921. In nine seasons with Chicago, Pittsburgh and Boston, "Whitey" stroked 1,340 hits, homered 48 times and drove in 747 runs.

Galesburg-born Jim Sundberg is probably the best-known Galesburg native son to play in the big leagues. Jim Howard Sundberg was born on May 18, 1951, in Galesburg and made his Major League debut with the Texas Rangers as a catcher on April 4, 1974. "Sunny" played sixteen seasons with Texas, Milwaukee, Kansas City and the Chicago Cubs. He played in

1,962 games, collecting 1,493 hits and 95 homers, drove in 624 runs and stole 20 bases. Jim Sundberg appeared in 3 All-Star games and earned 6 Gold Gloves as a catcher.

Mike Davison was born in Galesburg on August 4, 1945, and broke into the Major Leagues on October 1, 1969, as a pitcher with the San Francisco Giants. Davison pitched in thirty-two games over two seasons, winning three games and earning one save.

Although not born in Galesburg or the area, both Grover Cleveland Alexander and Evar Swanson honed their baseball skills in Galesburg. Alexander played his first professional game with a Galesburg minor league team and eventually was inducted into the Baseball Hall of Fame. Evar Swanson was a star athlete at Lombard College in Galesburg and still holds the Major League all-time speed record for "rounding the bases." Swanson also played professional football and served as Galesburg postmaster.

Record Basketball Freeze

The ending result of the basketball game between Lombard and Knox Colleges of Galesburg in December 1924 was considered one of the biggest farces in college roundball history. It would be a mighty stretch to compare the game to that which originated with a peach basket over a doorway.

The game was forecast as a tossup between two of the better college teams in the Midwest. The Galesburg Armory played host to the standing room only crowd. Lombard College featured Evar "Swanee" Swanson and Roy "Roddy" Lamb, who both would eventually excel in professional sports.

Lombard was considered one of the fastest teams in the country and proved it early. The Olives took the opening jump ball and scored within seconds. With a dazzling burst of speed, Lombard raced to an eleven to one lead during the first twelve minutes. The game appeared to be a runaway; however, no one in their wildest dreams could foresee what would occur.

The game took a complete reversal of form as Lombard teammates passed the ball around among themselves, never attempting a shot, and stalled away the final eight minutes of the first half. The score remained eleven to one in favor of Lombard at halftime. Knox College had only a mere free throw to show for its frustrating efforts.

Needless to say, the fans became very restless and irritated, venting their opinions rather freely, but they hadn't seen anything yet. When the second half resumed, Lombard controlled the tip and gave the ball to Evar Swanson. Swanee lodged the ball against his hip and proceeded to stand in place for seventeen consecutive minutes. At no time did Swanson attempt to pass off, and Knox College players made no attempt to steal the ball.

What occurred next has never been repeated in the history of basketball. The fans began to voice their disapproval in earnest and matters threatened to become a near riot. In an effort to restore peace, the Knox College student band played "The Star-Spangled Banner." Every person in the armory stood at attention, including Lombard player Evar Swanson, holding the ball, until the National Anthem was completed.

The atmosphere in the vast military hall took on that of a band concert as the Knox band played several more tunes. Meanwhile, Swanee's only move was to alternate the ball from one hip to the other. At the close of the impromptu band concert, Lombard finally put the ball into play; however, the damage was done. The game ended eleven to one, with neither team attempting a shot in the final twenty-eight minutes of the game.

The ghosts of the one-hundred-year-old armory on North Broad Street in Galesburg will likely never forget what occurred on the basketball court on a Wednesday night in December 1924.

PITCHER'S HELPER

If you watch baseball in only the slightest way, you will notice that there is only one piece of equipment lying loose in the field of play. It is the rosin or resin bag that is placed near the back of the pitcher's mound. Often during the course of a baseball game on any level, the pitcher picks up the rosin bag and slams it back to the ground.

The general definition of the rosin bag is "a bag filled with rosin; used by baseball pitchers to improve their grip on the ball. It is equipment used in playing baseball."

It was not until 1926 that a Major League baseball rules committee agreed that pitchers could have access to the rosin bag. Originally, the American League refused to permit its use. It finally gave in but discouraged use by its players.

Did you ever wonder how the ritual of a pitcher going to the rosin bag originated? It appears that a former Galesburg resident was the first player to use rosin as a pitching aid. Paul C. Mulberry, who resided on South Academy Street in the mid-1950s, was credited with using the white powder in 1916 during a game in Greene County, north of St. Louis.

During his younger days as a pitcher, Mulberry was having trouble controlling his curveball. One day when helping to thresh hay on the farm, he noticed that the farmer was applying a white powder to the fan belts of the threshing machine. Upon inquiry, he was told the substance was rosin. Mulberry speculated that the rosin powder might be the answer to his pitching problems. He purchased some of the rosin, which was a byproduct of turpentine. The next day, on July 31, 1916, he used the rosin during a game for the first time.

Mulberry, who was a Chicago Cub prospect, was certain he was the first baseball player ever to use rosin when pitching. What occurred during that game was a classic in itself. He hurled a no-hitter, striking out fifteen, and lost the game one to zero. The lone run was scored on a strikeout by Mulberry and unfortunately both the catcher and a fielder made wild throws, allowing the only run of the game to score.

Initially, Mulberry would dip his pitching fingers into the powder contained in a paper bag of his trouser pocket. He soon decided that the paper bag was not satisfactory and switched to a salt sack. Not surprisingly, the opposition eventually complained to the umpires and forced an investigation. The umpires decided the use of the rosin was acceptable but that the bag must be placed on the ground near the pitcher's mound.

Mulberry, who was originally from Bushnell, had his promising baseball career cut short during World War I when he contracted the flu and pneumonia, which settled in his pitching arm. The illness decreased the zip of his curveball. He felt that the secret of his curveball was the placing of the rosin on his fingers in a strategic place.

The conductors of the syndicated column and cartoon, Ripley's Believe It Or Not, believed that Paul Mulberry was the first to use the rosin bag during an actual baseball game. They featured his feat in nationwide newspapers during July 1954.

Olympic Gold

A curious reader inquired recently if an area person had ever participated in the World Olympics. The answer is yes, and not only did John "Jack" Whitman compete in the Olympics representing the United States, but he also brought home eleven gold medals.

Whitman was born and raised on a farm outside of Cameron, west of Galesburg. He was a 1948 graduate of Galesburg High School, where he starred in football and track for the Silver Streaks. His father, Harold Whitman, was a longtime member of the School District 205 Board of Education.

Jack became a student at the University of Illinois in 1949, where fate appeared to play a nasty trick on him. While participating with the Illini gymnastics squad, he suffered a freak accident that left him paralyzed from the waist down for the remainder of his life. After considerable rehab, Jack returned to the University of Illinois in 1952 through the rehabilitation education program for disabled students.

Determined to continue his dream of being a successful athlete, Jack took up archery. His newly discovered sport not only changed his life in a most positive fashion but also allowed him to leave his mark throughout the nation. Jack soon was recognized as the top wheelchair archer in the nation. In 1960, the former Silver Streak was selected as a member of the United States' Wheelchair Olympic team that would compete at Rome, Italy. Whitman won three gold medals in archery, thus becoming the first wheelchair athlete to win a gold medal. He also claimed the silver medal in table tennis.

Record performances are generally considered hard to come by for most athletes, but Whitman made them look routine. At the 1962 international games in Windsor, England, he set two new world records in archery by scoring 1,032 points, eclipsing the former mark of 832. A gold medal in archery followed during the 1963 Stoke Mandeville Games.

Jack was elected to the National Wheelchair Athletic Committee and served as the USA Wheelchair Archery coach from 1967 until 1976. His archery career was topped off in 1971, when he was inducted into the United States Wheelchair Sports Hall of Fame. Jack was recognized as America's father of wheelchair archery.

The 1948 Galesburg High and 1955 University of Illinois graduate also received several professional awards while serving as an advertising sales manager of radio and television stations in Champaign-Urbana. He died at his home in Champaign on September 30, 2004.

Jack Whitman never recognized that he lived with a handicap. Galesburg High School has recognized a multitude of graduates who have excelled in athletics and life in its hall of fame, but for some reason it appears that Whitman has slipped through the cracks.

THE GIZZ KIDS

When the Galesburg University of Illinois branch opened in 1947, the campus athletic program included both intercollegiate and intramural venues. The emergence of capable athletes resulted in competition with outside opponents in basketball, baseball and swimming. The intramural program included the participation of women and involved activities from ping-pong to football.

In early 1947, Doug Mills, the athletic director at the University of Illinois, called a press conference to announce the official formation of a basketball team on the Galesburg campus. F.T. Siewert, chairman of the physical education department, was appointed coach. The urgent call for prospects resulted in forty-two bodies showing up for tryouts. Home games would be played in the renovated campus gymnasium that would accommodate one thousand spectators. The new team would be nicknamed the Hurricanes.

The first game was played at the historic Alice Ingersoll Gym in Canton. The local University of Illinois won its opener thirty-five to twenty-three behind the scoring of Clint Cator. The Hurricanes won their first ever home game by defeating the Knox College B team fifty-one to thirty-four. Harry Johnson scored the first basket and the first free throw in what is now known as the Hawthorne Gym. Russell "Bucky" Swise, who had starred in athletics at Galesburg High and Knox College, officiated the inaugural home game. Students were admitted to the game free, family members were charged twenty-five cents and townspeople were admitted for fifty cents.

The Galesburg team included Harry Johnson from Woodriver, Clint Cator from Belividere, Don Feldman from Geneseo, Bill Barry from Monmouth and Rich Meyers from Mendon. Coach Siewart was a former college star at Wittenburg and had played professional basketball.

During the second year of operation, both baseball and swimming were added as competitive sports. Gar Braun coached the first baseball team and had the luxury of choosing from eighty-four prospects. The local branch lost its opener to Eureka five to four but bounced back for its first victory, defeating Monmouth seven to six in extra innings. Jack Savidge from Galesburg was a member of the first baseball team. Savidge would become a prominent national referee.

The second year of basketball saw most of the players returning and was enhanced with the addition of Ray Hendricks, who had played for Galesburg High School. Hendricks led the Hurricanes in scoring by averaging ten points per game. In a loss to Western State Teachers College from Macomb, Hendricks scored a game-high fourteen points. Former Streak George Lundeen led Macomb with ten points. Galesburg played Quincy College and was matched up with El and Mel Tappe, who would play and coach the Chicago Cubs.

The University of Illinois campus at Galesburg was not able to match the athletic programs offered at the mother campus; however, a program that would set the standard nationwide for paraplegic sports was initiated here. The University of Illinois Fighting Illini wheelchair basketball team was formally organized on the Galesburg campus in 1948 and aptly named the "Gizz Kids." The wheelchair team was the first collegiate team in the United States. Games on the Galesburg campus were played before standing room only crowds and led to moving many games to the Galesburg Armory.

The Gizz Kids hosted the first ever National Invitational Wheelchair Basketball Tournament in March 1949. Teams from Indiana, Missouri, Minnesota and Chicago joined the Gizz Kids. Kansas City won the tourney and Galesburg finished third. All games were broadcast on WGIL and covered by newspapers and wire services nationally.

Although most games were played with other paraplegic teams, it was common to schedule games with local all-stars. In December 1948, the Gizz Kids defeated local former collegiate stars forty to twenty. The opponents, who were not used to playing basketball while being forced to operate a wheelchair, included Knox standouts Jim Pogue and Bill Heerde. Galesburg High coach and former Illini "Whiz Kid" Ken Menke also participated.

XX on Simmons Street

"There is no tomorrow for many in the sports world" read a headline in newspapers throughout the county on January 16, 1959. The story that followed revealed that Jimmy Foxx, one of baseball's all-time greats, was nearly penniless.

Jimmy, or Jimmie, Foxx was described as "not a perfect man, but a good man, generous and respected, liked and loved by many and a hell of a ballplayer." Foxx broke into the baseball Major Leagues as a catcher with the Philadelphia Athletics at the age of seventeen. During his twenty-year Major League career, Foxx hit 534 homers, 1,922 runs batted in and finished with a career .325 batting average. His twelve consecutive seasons with 30 or more home runs was a Major League record until it was broken by Barry Bonds in 2004. Foxx was voted the American League MVP on three occasions and was inducted into baseball's Hall of Fame in 1951.

The 1959 national newspaper article depicting the unfortunate plight of Jimmie Foxx was fortunately read by Galesburg restaurateur Nunzio "Nunc" Mangieri, which led to a major change in Foxx's life. Nunc and his brother Tony, along with business partner Joe Donato, sent a telegram to Foxx and offered him a chance to manage a restaurant in Galesburg. Foxx said, "There's no kiddin' about it, I needed a job." Foxx visited Galesburg, liked what he saw and within a few months he was operating a restaurant bearing his name at 232 East Simmons Street. The plush Jimmie Foxx Restaurant opened its doors on August 26, 1959. The menu featured open hearth charcoal steaks and a noonday buffet luncheon for $1.10 per person. The decor included Foxx's uniforms, bats and trophies from his illustrious baseball career. A full-page ad in the *Galesburg Register-Mail* announced the grand opening of the Foxx Restaurant on November 4, 1959. Foxx received congratulatory telegrams wishing him the best in his new venture from baseball personalities Joe DiMaggio, Ted Williams, Hank Greenburg, Bill Veeck, Gabby Hartnett and Stan Musial.

One of the frequent visitors to the Foxx Restaurant was Galesburg postmaster Evar Swanson, who also was a former Major League baseball star. As reported in a "Tracking History" column, Foxx brought former Negro League baseball player Eddie Thompson with him to manage the food operations. Foxx, then fifty-one years old, was accompanied to Galesburg by his wife Dorothy and fifteen-year-old son Jim. Jim attended Churchill Jr. High School and played baseball in the Galesburg Junior Hardball League.

Jimmie Foxx was plagued with what seemed to be constant bad luck during his stay in Galesburg. Shortly after the restaurant's opening, Foxx was laid low by what was described as a mild heart attack. He had taken his wife Dorothy to the Bondi Building office of Dr. Howard Graham for a treatment of a sprained wrist when he fainted. Foxx spent several days in the hospital catching up on his reading and TV Westerns. The setback caused a delay in the grand opening of the restaurant.

Unfortunately, after only one year of operation, Jimmie Foxx struck out in his Galesburg restaurant venture. Owners Joe Donato and Nunzio and Tony Mangieri decided not to renew Foxx's contract. Not only was Double X out of a job, but he was also forced to apply for unemployment compensation, which would be thirty-five dollars weekly. Foxx was quoted as saying, "I'm broke, and I guess I always will be." Nunzio Mangieri commented, "Jimmie was one of the most talented handlers of people I have ever seen. The failure of the restaurant was no fault of Jimmie's."

After applying for unemployment compensation, Foxx received several job offers. Again, bad luck struck as Foxx suffered a concussion and severe skull fracture when he fell down the basement stairs at his house in Galesburg. Foxx, whose life had more ups and downs than a left-field bounder, died July 21, 1967.

A few years ago, a baseball autographed by Jimmie Foxx appeared on an online auction list. The ball was stamped with "The Jimmy Foxx restaurant" on one section and sold for over $2,000. In March 2000, a 1934 Goudey Jimmy Foxx No. 1 baseball card topped the Collectors Universe Superior Sports spring auction with a final hammer price of $31,050.

How many of you were fortunate enough to obtain an autograph or even a souvenir menu from Jimmie Foxx at his restaurant on Simmons Street?

CHAPTER 6

IT REALLY HAPPENED

FOUGHT CHICAGO FIRE

Inquiries from readers of the "Tracking History" column about Galesburg history have been interesting, to say the least. Recently, a reader inquired if the Galesburg Fire Department had provided mutual aid to Chicago during the Great Fire of October 8, 1871.

The *Galesburg Republican Register* newspaper of October 14, 1871, highlighted news of the tragic fire on its front page. The report described that Chicago was in ashes, there were scenes of terror and over three miles of fire and nearly eight hundred acres were burned over. The opening paragraph declared that the fire was the most disastrous conflagration that had ever occurred on this continent.

The best of the city of Chicago was destroyed, including the post office, printing plants, the waterworks, hotels, theatres, city hall and hundreds of homes. The Galesburg newspaper reported that a large and enthusiastic meeting was held at the opera house to make arrangements for collecting provisions and clothing for the relief of those left homeless during the fire. The meeting was called to order by Galesburg mayor Timothy Nash. A committee consisting of George W. Foote, George Ekins, George Davis, A. Knowles and Mr. Lewis was formed to coordinate solicitation of needed commodities. It was announced that C.S. and Francis Colton had delivered a large amount of clothing to the depot and had pledged fifty dollars as well. Officer Smith announced that he had received a dispatch from Clark E. Carr that he was contributing thirty-five dollars. Judge Alfred Knowles said he would contribute one barrel of flour and twenty-five dollars. G.V. Dieterich ordered two barrels of flour baked into bread. An announcement was made that six dray loads of provisions and clothing were at the depot for immediate shipping to Chicago. Judge Kitchell volunteered to pick up by car any boxes left at local grocery establishments. Each announcement was followed by a loud standing ovation.

Mayor Nash announced that he had appointed two extra night policemen to guard the provisions left at the depot for shipping. It was announced that all Galesburg bakeries would operate all night as long as needed to ensure that as much cooked food as possible could be sent. It was apparent that the fine railroad facilities and numerous daily trains to Chicago made Galesburg an important and strategic point for aiding victims of the Chicago fire.

Near the conclusion of the meeting, a request was made to ask the Galesburg City Council to appropriate $1,000 for the immediate relief of the Chicago sufferers.

Yes, the city of Galesburg did indeed provide mutual fire aid to the city of Chicago. The Galesburg City Council authorized sending a fire engine and a crew of men to Chicago with intentions to aid in fighting the fire. The minutes of the city council meeting on October 9, 1871, "resolved that the Mayor be authorized to expend such sum as in his discretion may send equipment in extending immediate aid to the sufferers by the Chicago fire not exceeding in amount $500."

Members of the Galesburg City Council who authorized aid to the Chicago Fire Department included M.E. Fuller, George H. Smith, Edwin Knowles, J.P. Chapman, Sam Hitchcock, James Cleary and B.F. Arnold. A City of Galesburg Ordinance Book didn't list a fire marshal until 1939, when Earl E. Cratty was noted.

We are indebted to current Galesburg fire chief John Cratty for furnishing information about the mutual aid to Chicago. Chief Cratty also revealed that the city council passed an ordinance creating the Galesburg Fire Department on February 24, 1858. The 150th anniversary of the Galesburg Fire Department was in February 2008.

CIRCUS SURPRISE

History reveals that many of the famous traveling circuses performed in Galesburg in the early 1900s. The granddaddy of them all, the famous Barnum & Bailey Circus, made annual visits to Galesburg as early as 1907. Many notable actors and cowboys made special appearances, including Tom Mix and the original speaking Lone Ranger, Lee Powell.

On June 12, 1917, the Sells-Floto Circus train pulled into Galesburg and unloaded on North Broad Street at the site of the Santa Fe freight

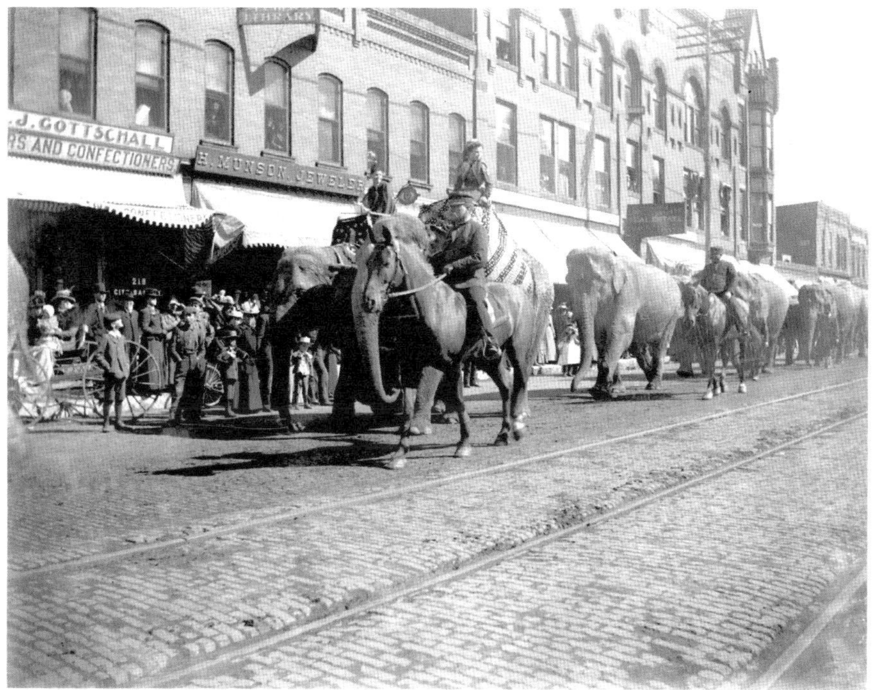

Sells-Floto Circus parade in downtown Galesburg, early 1900s. A baby elephant was born in Galesburg during a circus appearance.

depot. Hundreds of area residents were up bright and early to witness the appearance of elephants, camels and special show horses. As was usual for many years, the circus proceeded down East Main Street to the vast green lot that Interstate 74 now covers at the city's eastern edge.

Between dawn and noon, a white city of tents covered the eleven acres of green space, which was owned by the Swanson family. Next came the gala circus parade downtown. It was one of the longest and brightest ever seen in this area. The circus vehicles were bright and new and the circus folk were clad in red, white and blue patriotic garb. Five splendid bands of music were sandwiched between other features in the line of march.

The animal display was especially interesting, with dozens of full-view cages showing off the lions and tigers. More than three hundred of the finest show horses, in all colors from snow white to jet black, pranced to martial music. Thirty-five jolly clowns mounted on Rocky Mountain burros produced much laughter, especially among the youngsters.

A special attraction of the parade was the appearance of boxing's first Triple World Champion, Bob Fitzsimmons. The colorful boxer would appear later during the circus performance in an exhibition match with his twenty-one-year-old son, who was challenging for the heavyweight world championship. Sadly, the elder Fitzsimmons would die a short time after the Galesburg appearance.

Indeed, the appearance of the Sells-Floto Circus was to be long remembered by area residents, but not for originally publicized reasons. Oquawka was placed on the tourism map in 1972 when a circus elephant named Norma Jean was struck by lightning and died on the spot. A handsome memorial gravesite in Oquawka now pays honor to the fallen elephant. But Oquawka really has nothing on Galesburg when it comes to elephant stories.

The largest elephant and the star of the Sells-Floto Circus was named Bebbo. Unfortunately, the star did not appear in the parade down Main Street nor, for that matter, did she perform during the gala three-ring show. Bebbo enjoyed a day of leisure while in Galesburg. In the morning, her caretaker took her for a leisurely stroll through the woods east of Galesburg.

Late in the afternoon, Bebbo, in her very expensive private car, presented the Sells-Floto Circus and the residents of Galesburg with a new addition to the herd. Shortly after the new calf was born, Bebbo was nicknamed Mother Marie. Amazingly, the birth was the first for Mother Marie and she was fifty-three years old.

The Sells-Floto Circus owners established a record in the cost of childbirth. For over two months it cost them twenty dollars per day for a special car to house the expectant mother, as it was not feasible to keep her with the rest of the herd. The hundreds of pounds of green food and hay added to the daily cost.

Records at the time of birth established that this was indeed the first elephant ever born to a circus performing in the United States and, for sure, the first one ever born in Galesburg. It would seem a safe bet to assume that the baby of Bebbo is still the only elephant ever born in Galesburg.

A CHARMED LIFE

On Sunday evening, April 14, 1913, a wall caved in at the historical Lindell House Hotel on Depot Street near the Knox College campus. Originally known as the American Hotel, it was a stopover for Abraham Lincoln and Stephen Douglas during their Galesburg visits, being situated next door to the original Burlington Railroad Depot. Miraculously, no one was hurt; however, a nearby shoe shop was demolished and it caused great panic among its boarders. Most of the residents were foreigners employed at the Burlington Tie Plant.

The manager of the hotel/boardinghouse, Frank "Franz" Karun (often spelled Kurun or Korun), barely escaped being trapped in the rubble. Karun, who was thirty-nine years old, was from Slovenia and resided in the Lindell House with his wife and five children.

The fact that Frank Karun escaped injury or death during the building's collapse likely confirmed that he was born under a lucky star. There was indeed a very peculiar circumstance in connection with the building's collapse. It was exactly one year earlier to the day and hour, April 14, 1912, that the famed *Titanic* ship hit an iceberg and sank. The tragic accident was the worst peacetime maritime disaster in history, resulting in the death of 1,517 passengers.

The *Titanic*, which surpassed all rivals in luxury and opulence, began its maiden voyage from Southampton, England, bound for New York City on April 12, 1912. Among the passengers were Frank Karun, his four-year-old daughter Manca and his wife's brother, John Markum. Karun was returning from his homeland after selling the family farm for $750, all of which was lost when the *Titanic* sank. The threesome boarded the ill-fated *Titanic* at Cherbourg as third-class passengers. Karun related that he picked out the best boat so they could enjoy the trip back to America better. It is probably becoming obvious that Frank Karun and his four-year-old daughter were two of the only 706 who survived the sinking of the *Titanic*. In fact, Karun was among only a few males, as most survivors were women and small children.

Both the *Galesburg Republican Register* and the *Galesburg Evening Mail* published extensive descriptions of the father and daughter's experiences in surviving the tragedy. These reports contained many errors and conflicting details because of very difficult media communication problems during that time period.

Karun, who spoke broken English, described that he was asleep when the *Titanic* struck the iceberg. He was in the third-class sleeping room at the rear of the boat with his daughter and brother-in-law, John Markum. When they quickly dressed and got to the deck, they could see that the forward end of the boat was sinking. There was a lifeboat lowered, which might have been the last one, and Karun's daughter was placed in the boat first. Karun was the last to be lowered by rope, which greatly surprised him, since all the rest of the bystanders were women and children. There were fifty-two people on the rescue boat.

Karun related that they spent nearly five hours in the rescue boat in freezing temperatures. They were fortunate to be rescued and placed aboard the rescue ship *Carpathia*. Upon arrival of the rescue ship in New York, Karun and his daughter were taken to St. Vincent's Hospital. They spent two and a half days in the hospital, eventually returning to Galesburg on a Burlington train at 10:00 p.m. on April 22.

In 1914, the Karun family returned to Austria/Slovenia. Manca (the daughter who survived the *Titanic* tragedy with her father) had four siblings who returned to the United States and lived out their lives in America.

Frank "Franz" Karun died in Milje, Slovenia, on July 7, 1934.

Comedian Apparently Slept Here

Much evidence exists that a multitude of famous stage performers graced the stages of Galesburg theatres around the turn of the century. Convenient train travel through the city and the existence of the Auditorium Theatre on Broad and Ferris Streets enabled residents to enjoy the best of the best onstage.

The famous theatre just off the Public Square hosted the Marx Brothers, and history has it that their legendary nicknames came about during an onstage poker game in the palace that was later tabbed the opera house.

One of the most notable entertainers to grace the opera house was comedian and juggler W.C. Fields. Now there is much evidence that W.C. spent more time entertaining off the stage while in Galesburg. The reputed lover of alcoholic beverages was born William Claude Dukenfield on January 29, 1880, in Philadelphia. Fields dropped out of school in the fourth grade after logging a dismal attendance record.

Details of Fields's life through his mid-teens are in dispute but a former Galesburg resident attempted to fill in the missing links. An Associated Press story that appeared in the *Register-Mail* on January 26, 1951, presented some evidence that the comedian might have married while only thirteen years old.

Mrs. Edith Williams, seventy-one years old at the time of the article, filed suit to recover support monies, claiming Fields had fathered seven children with her and abandoned them in Galesburg. Edith Williams claimed that she had married the bulb-nosed funny man in 1893 when she was only thirteen years old. Mrs. Williams indicated that Fields also used the names Bill Williams and William Ward. It was purported that he claimed to be Bill Williams during his alleged escapades with Edith.

Edith Williams initially filed a petition for letters of administration in Chicago probate court during December 1950, claiming that W.C. had $50,000 in Illinois property. Mrs. Williams, who was nearly blind at the time of the petition, claimed that five sons from her marriage were still alive.

Fields unfortunately fought various illnesses throughout his life and finally succumbed on Christmas Day 1946 in Pasadena, California. Although the official cause of death was listed as pneumonia, it was all related to his constant drinking.

Following Fields's death, a battle royal was waged between various claimants, including Edith Fields from Galesburg. In 1899, during a performance in New York City, W.C. had met a dancer named Harriet (Hattie) Hughes and they were married shortly thereafter. Another lover, Carlotta Monti, also became party to the circus of claims.

It appears that Edith Fields was left in the cold in her attempt to claim a portion of Fields's estate. A settlement in the extensive and bitterly contested litigation was granted on January 19, 1951, in California. Fields's widow, Harriet, was awarded the majority of the funds. Strangely, William Rexford Fields Morris, a Dallas airline clerk, was awarded $15,000. The Texan claimed to be the illegitimate son of W.C. and the late Follies dancer Bessie Poole.

Attempts to determine the fate of Edith Fields and her surviving sons have proved unsuccessful at this point. There is some evidence that Edith worked as a salesperson at the O.T. Johnson Big Store.

Stop!

Galesburg vehicle drivers don't always believe in signs—at least not stop signs. I admit that one of my main pet peeves is watching Galesburg area drivers blow through stop signs. Recently I asked a local law enforcement officer why people disobey stop signs. His feelings were that the infractions increased when "right-hand turns on red" were permitted. Stop signs are posted to reduce collisions and show motorists who has the right of way. They are intended to evenly distribute vehicles entering an intersection.

Recently, a national poll revealed reasons why people have such a high disregard for stopping: "Other motorists do not obey stop signs so why should I?" "I can drive however I like, so long as I avoid hitting another car or pedestrian." "The law does not apply to me." "Obeying stop signs is too much work, when you stop you have to work extra hard to get back up to speed." And finally, "I like speed. I do not want to go for a ride where I have to stop and start…over and over again."

I was delighted to read recently that the *Galesburg Register-Mail* was also curious about the failure to obey stop signs. A *Register-Mail* reporter was assigned to visit several stop sign crossings and obtain statistics on the number of cars not stopping. The reporter's assignment was limited to four intersections on Prairie Street. Half-hour readings were conducted at Prairie and Ferris, Prairie and North, Prairie and Grove and Prairie and Fremont.

About one-third of motor vehicles approaching the crossings completely ignored the stop signs, and 32 percent failed to come to a complete stop, but continued to move all the time. It was noted that the majority of those running the stop signs were men and young boys. Many of the youngsters driving were under age to have a license and most disobeyed stopping. The reporter concluded that although no accidents were witnessed, female drivers coasting through the stop signs came the nearest to having collisions.

The *Register-Mail* reporter witnessed that thirty-one out of fifty-eight vehicles either ran signs or coasted through the intersection of Prairie and Ferris. At Prairie and North, nine out of twenty-four failed to stop completely and another nine coasted through the intersection. Fifteen out of nineteen vehicles failed to stop at Prairie and Fremont.

Even though I much appreciated the *Register-Mail* assigning a reporter to check out the blatant disregard for a particular driving law, it seemed appropriate that I conduct my own survey. I sat patiently in my auto at Prairie and North and was shocked at the results. Of the 68 drivers who crossed Prairie from North Street, 23 ran the stop signs big time and another 25 coasted through at best. Strangely enough, a bicyclist ran the stop sign and was nearly sandwiched by autos going each way on Prairie. The big shocker was to witness a young bike rider coming to a complete stop before proceeding. It should also be noted that 4 drivers proceeded across the railroad tracks when the gates were going down near the North Street intersection. At the four-way stop intersection where Prairie and Ferris Streets cross, 76 of 163 vehicles failed to obey the traffic stop sign.

What does this all mean? It is obvious that I witnessed much more traffic than the *Register-Mail* reporter, and you should wonder why. Should any of these statistics really concern you with all the things going on in our lives? Is this subject a pet peeve of anyone else?

Just for the record, and hopefully to put all of this possible nonsense in perspective, the *Register-Mail* did indeed send a reporter to observe stop sign happenings at four Prairie Street intersections. Indeed, I did use my lunch hour to observe some of the same locations. Strangely enough, the *Register-Mail* reporter was sent to Prairie Street stop sign corners during July 1931, over seventy-seven years ago. Now you might understand the reason I observed more traffic. Another thing I observed would not have been possible for the *Register-Mail* reporter to see: the running of a stop sign while talking on a cellphone.

Galesburg Boys Sit It Out

Although the following notes on past Galesburg history were not earth shattering or likely to be placed in the *Guinness Book of World Records*, they were too unique to pass up. Marathon endurance contests are legendary, including dance contests, pole sitting and so on. Several Galesburg boys attempted in 1930 to set the national tree sitting record, and a former resident set out to prove he could sit in a motorboat longer than anyone ever.

During July 1930, a national craze of tree sitting caused quite a buzz throughout the land, including in Galesburg. Charles Hanlin, age sixteen, and his buddy John Meiers, age twelve, climbed into a tree at Hanlin's home at 123 West Third Street on July 15. Across town, two sixteen-year-old boys, Rex Holcomb and Harrison Gates, were perched high in a giant tree in front of the Holcomb residence at 362 Maple Avenue. A third team joined the fray, picking out a large elm tree west of the Knox College Gym. The additional competitors were Ralph Thielbert, age thirteen, of 46 South Cedar Street, and fifteen-year-old Frances Moats of 676 West Tompkins Street.

Hundreds of curious townspeople showed up daily to chat with the tree sitters and offer encouragement. Hanlin and Meiers announced to onlookers that they planned to remain aloft until all other competitors had given up. Gates and Holcomb had a cardboard sign nailed to their tree stating that they intended to remain perched in the tree for at least 368 hours and that no contributions would be refused. When young Gates was asked by a *Register-Mail* reporter how long he intended to stay aloft, his sharp reply was, "You will be gray haired by the time we come down!"

It became obvious that the boys' and girl's ability to rest at night was more successful than that of their parents. A neighbor of Hanlin chained the children to a platform nightly, retaining the key and not releasing them until morning. Holcomb and Gates passed the time by doing chores for their parents, including shelling green beans. Hanlin and Meiers were not as industrious as their competitors, as they refused to wash and dry dishes from their tree perch. They passed the time by reading and playing checkers.

As the local youths passed the four-day mark, reports were received from all parts of the country on the status of other tree sitters. Many onlookers made financial contributions to the boys, with one local man offering five dollars to each one who passed the one-hundred-hour mark. College City Dairy supplied each boy with a quart of milk and ice cream treats daily. A Galesburg barber offered free haircuts to each lad when they returned to mother earth. It should be noted that Harry Palmer and LeRoy McCollough served as the refueling crew for Hanlin and Meiers.

Howard Barry and Mickey Holcomb took care of arrangements for Gates and Holcomb.

The tree sitting contest came to an abrupt end on the ninth day at high noon. An agreement was reached to terminate the sitting and the boys did not sponsor it. It was enacted by arrangements finalized by their parents. No doubt the rivalry formed by the boys would have dragged on for several weeks. To put it simply, constant watching and the curious visitors wore out the parents.

Meanwhile, publicity was received from Cleveland, Ohio, that a former Galesburg resident was attempting to set a longtime mark of staying in a motorboat. The world's record of 118 hours and 49 minutes had been set the week before and George Mishey was attempting to top the mark. Local fans remembered Mishey for his pitching efforts when he starred with Lombard College and the Galesburg Indies. Fans recalled that George could make a baseball game almost an endurance contest by endless hitching of his belt, glaring at the catcher and looking to the sky before deciding what to throw. Former friends were of the opinion that if George could move as slowly as he pitched, a motorboat endurance record was in sight.

ROARS THROUGH TOWN

During the early 1900s, the name of Walter Edward Scott, more popularly known as "Death Valley Scotty," appeared nearly daily in newspapers throughout the country. Scotty came about because of reports that he had made an enormous gold strike. Whether he actually struck it rich was continually debated; however, he appeared to always have plenty of money to spend and he usually spent it in spectacular ways.

In July 1905, Scotty received nationwide publicity by claiming he would break the cross-country train speed record. On Sunday afternoon, July 9, at 1:00 p.m., he departed from Los Angeles for Chicago on a special train called the Death Valley Coyote that consisted of an engine, baggage car, a sleeper and a dining car. The only passengers were Scotty, his wife Ella and several reporters.

Early in the morning of July 11, a dispatch was received that the special would stop in Galesburg long enough to pick up a bundle of newspapers. It was estimated that over four hundred people were at the Santa Fe Depot, hopeful that they would get a good look at Death Valley Scotty. The track was cleared for the special at 8:40 a.m. and it was exactly 8:51 a.m. when the excited spectators heard the shrill whistle of Engine 510 coming from the vicinity of the coal chutes.

The next instant, the engine and train rounded the curve and whipped by the passenger depot and out of sight on its way to Chicago. Unfortunately, the special failed to make a perceptible stop in Galesburg as scheduled. The train traveled the fifty-five miles from Fort Madison, Iowa, to Galesburg in exactly fifty-one minutes, thus maintaining the claim of traveling "a mile a minute."

The special train reached Chicago at 11:54 a.m., six minutes ahead of the fastest estimate to break the world record. It was probably best that the train failed to stop in Galesburg, since the special was laid over in Chillicothe for six minutes on account of a hot box. Death Valley Scotty and his Death Valley Coyote train traveled the distance of 2,264 miles in forty-four hours and fifty-four minutes, with two hours being deducted for change in time.

Scotty boasted, "We got there so fast that nobody had time to sober up!" Although he failed to stop in Galesburg during the record train run, he had appeared with the Buffalo Bill Cody Wild West Show at the local circus grounds at the age of sixteen.

One Warning Omitted

In March 1943, the Illinois secretary of state announced that new plastic automobile plates were being issued to take the place of metal ones as a war conservation aid.

A warning was issued to take care when attaching them to the car because they were easily breakable and should be placed so that they couldn't easily be bumped into. One warning that the state official failed to issue was "to not park your car in a hog confinement lot." Apparently there was something in the plastic composition that hogs were fond of.

Meanwhile, in the Monmouth rural area, a farmer parked his truck in the barn lot and soon discovered that the hogs had devoured his license plates. Although the secretary of state was very skeptical when informed of the calamity, he admitted that apparently too many soybeans were used in making the plates.

Improbable but True

Occasionally events happen that seem improbable or even impossible. Although not necessarily of great historical value, they nevertheless are mind-boggling.

His Death Exaggerated!

In early January 1946, nearly sixty-four years ago, a Galesburg man strongly objected to his published funeral plans. Chuck, who resided on Galesburg's south side, was shocked to read his own obituary in the *Register-Mail* while still a patient at a Galesburg hospital. The astonishing event resulted from an unfortunate error by the hospital staff.

Chuck shared a hospital room with Dave, a Knox County farmer who resided north of Galesburg. A hospital attendant mistakenly notified Chuck's brother of his death. Knowing his brother had heart problems and had been in serious condition, he ordered the deceased be moved to a local undertaking establishment. The following morning, the family visited the funeral home, made final burial plans and provided information for the newspaper obituary.

Early that evening, Chuck phoned his sister-in-law and announced that he was indeed very much alive. Needless to say, the astonished woman nearly fainted. Chuck explained that he had been reading the newspaper and came across the account of his death. In the meantime, hospital officials began an investigation and realized the impossible had actually occurred.

Members of the Knox County farmer's family were understandably overwhelmed by the tragic turn of affairs. A daughter residing in another state had visited Dave at the hospital and, thinking he was much improved, left for home. The positive development was that Chuck recovered from the ordeal and was soon released from the hospital.

Double Divorce

In July 1932, about seventy-eight years ago, a very novel case came up before Knox County judge Riley E. Stevens. Two Galesburg men, Eddie and Lee, both secured divorces in a most unusual fashion. According to bills filed in the cases, a local woman named Myrtle, with several aliases, had married Eddie here in 1920. Shortly thereafter, Myrtle ran away with Lee and went through a marriage ceremony in Frankfort, Kentucky. Several years later, she returned to Galesburg with Lee and was arrested and charged with giving herself to adulterous practices. Thus, Judge Stevens granted Eddie a divorce on grounds of adultery and Lee was granted the same on grounds that he was never legally married. Consequently, Eddie and Lee were granted divorces from the same woman.

Confined in Luxury

Galesburg's neighbor to the west, Monmouth, checks in with a bizarre happening from more than seventy-five years ago in 1933. The headline in the Galesburg paper read "Woman Serving Prison Term Surrounds Herself with Comforts of Ritz." Jennie was sentenced to a six-month term in the Warren County Jail for a variety of infractions. It was quickly apparent that jail life for Jennie was akin to a stay at a luxurious hotel resort.

Due to the fact that she would be the only woman confined to jail, the confinement could only be served in the jail's second-floor medical facilities, which were actually a large, comfortable apartment. The facilities included a private bath with hot and cold water. The young, pretty prisoner reported for confinement quite well dressed. Since the jail didn't own appropriate feminine uniforms, Jennie brought so much clothing with her that authorities were forced to provide an adjoining holding cell as a wardrobe area. The petite blonde made several trips daily to the wardrobe area to change her attire, claiming this was her only means of exercise.

Would you believe that friends were allowed to bring special pillows, curtains, bright rugs and shaded lamps to spruce up the decor? Ever wonder why people consider some jails to resemble country clubs?

City's Big Blazes

Quite often, structure fires in Galesburg during the past 150-plus years have turned into large spectator gatherings. It is difficult to find a single positive about a building burning, especially if there is a loss of life. We often hear the question, what was the most spectacular fire in Galesburg history? Or, what fire had the most negative effect psychologically on the community? Galesburg has lost a stately railroad depot, a high school building, a historic library, hotels, manufacturing plants, churches and a multitude of retail structures to tragic fires.

A case can be built that one of the most devastating fires in the community's history occurred fifty years ago on the evening of May 9, 1958. This fire destroyed the historic public library on East Simmons Street. The downtown was full of activity with Friday night shoppers and the library was experiencing heavy traffic from book browsers. As the fire progressed, the streets adjacent to the library were filled with over five thousand curious and shaken onlookers. Many of the saddened spectators had tears in their eyes as flames licked hundreds of feet into the skies. They watched as over 200,000 volumes, most of which were irreplaceable, went up in flames.

The library fire was discovered when black curling smoke was spotted in the attic of the landmark two-story structure. As librarians quickly hustled everyone safely out of the building, the firemen charged up the stairs, aiming hoses at the heart of the visible flames. Due to an unfortunate shortage of water pressure, only a dribble came out of the fire hoses. Within minutes, the flames spread unchecked through the attic and the roof collapsed. All that remained late into the night were naked walls of the once stately structure.

Although the structure by that time was only a whisper of its original use, word of the fire at the O.T. Johnson Big Store building early in the morning of January 23, 2006, was quickly relayed around the country. No doubt a thick book could be written about the memories of both the fire and the Big Store's magical history. Most residents were sound asleep when firefighters arrived in the 100 block of East Main Street to investigate a reported blaze that will undoubtedly live in people's minds forever. Tragically, the fire not only destroyed the three-story landmark department store building and four-story rear annex, but it also resulted in the death of local resident Michael Olson.

On Sunday, April 13, 1904, a $100,000 fire destroyed the two-story structure housing Galesburg High School and resulted in the death of two firemen. Losing their lives fighting the school blaze and adjacent kindergarten normal unit were John Slater of the City Fire Department and Frank Stromstedt of the CB&Q fire squad. It was only the second time in Galesburg history that a firefighter lost a life while on duty. On the other occasion, fireman Sutherland met death fighting the Union Hotel Fire in 1871. The building that replaced the 1904 fire at the corner of South Broad and Tompkins Streets also burned down while empty in the early 1960s.

An early afternoon blaze on December 14, 1908, destroyed the upper two floors of the Holmes Building at the corner of Main and Prairie Streets in downtown Galesburg. Numerous occupants narrowly escaped the building, including a woman who leaped from a fourth-story window to the roof of an adjoining building. One of the most hair-raising escapes was that of Dr. E.D. Wing, who had offices on the fourth floor. Unable to exit by elevator or the stairs, he climbed out a window and stood on a narrow concrete ledge until firemen raised an extension ladder to him. Verne Brown, an employee of the ground floor Continental Clothing Store, was one of the heroes. He took charge of the elevator and ran it until everyone was seemingly safely out of the building.

Galesburg firefighters displayed great courage and one of their most stellar efforts to confine a raging fire that gutted the three-story Labor Temple building at 52 North Prairie Street on April 3, 1962. The Labor Temple occupied the two top floors and the Louis Nyman Sporting Goods & Toy Store was on the ground floor. The fire, which threatened several nearby buildings, including the O.T. Johnson Big Store, also forced six women to vacate the next building north. One of the women, Louise Jones, widow of "Casey" Jones, who had been editor of the *Register-Mail*, discovered the fire.

It was a baptism for seventeen recently sworn-in firemen, who were credited by Fire Chief Wayne Nelson with saving adjacent buildings. All off-duty firemen were called in, allowing a force of forty-seven men. The department also was aided by firefighters from Monmouth and the Galesburg State Research Hospital. It was one year earlier that the two-story Hart Furniture Store across the street from the Labor Temple had gone up in roaring flames.

The first fire of note reported in Galesburg occurred in 1843, when the Female Seminary on South Seminary Street burned to the ground. The secondary school for female college students was considered one of the community's most stately buildings at the time. The three-story wooden structure was topped with a shining tin cupola that could be seen for miles on a sunny day. One of the costliest and most dangerous fires in early history occurred in 1923, when the Galesburg Horse and Mule Barn was destroyed. The block-long structure was adjacent to the Galesburg Armory between Broad and Cherry Streets. More than two hundred tons of hay stored in the upper portion were completely lost. Thousands of spectators descended on the scene as twenty horses were led to safety in the nick of time.

One of the most publicized fires occurred on November 12, 1958, when an early morning fire destroyed the popular Peerless Market on the northeast corner of Main Street and the Public Square. The upper floors of the structure contained several apartments, including one occupied by Helen Lescher Bessolo. Mrs. Bessolo was rescued by the fire department's hook and ladder truck and her seven pet dogs were saved by the efforts of nearby restaurant owner Barney McKay. A headline in the *Register-Mail* inquired, "Where Was Superman When His Mother Needed Him?" Helen Lescher Bessolo was the mother of George Reeves, who portrayed Superman in movies and television.

CHAPTER 7

A ZOO

The Saga of Matilda

An article in my "Tracking History" column featured Leonard H. Woods, who won the National Left Handers' Senior Golf Tourney in 1958. Three years later, the southpaw golfer, who also owned the Galesburg Order Buyers, authored a classic article in the *Register-Mail* after convincing the newspaper staff that his yarn was worth substituting for his weekly market review.

After reading the article that appeared in the August 11, 1961 issue of the *Register-Mail*, it struck me that it merited being retold. After several phone calls, we were able to verify that the "precious" story was not a fluke. We were fortunate to contact Mike Grady of Knoxville, who was a key participant in the rescue of Matilda.

Once upon a time in the village of Knox Station, near Knoxville, there lived a family who owned a pet pig by the name of Matilda. No doubt Matilda was a very intelligent little pig and soon discovered that most pigs eventually went to market, while pet pigs stayed home and lived the Life of Riley.

Life was easy and very pleasant for Matilda. She played with the kiddies and grunted happily while growing into a fine specimen of adulthood. When Matilda finally grew up, her human family decided it was time to find her a husband. There were many boy pigs around Knox Station but none in Matilda's class. Eventually the family talked with the Clyde Grady family, who lived on a farm in the Lake Rice area. It was learned that the Gradys possessed a pig called Strong Loin that would welcome Matilda, with the object being matrimony.

So Matilda left her happy home in Knox Station, passed through East Galesburg and finally arrived at Strong Loin's house on the eastern border of the lake known as Rice. Although Matilda appeared happy to be with Strong Loin, she could not forget her previous home and hoped to soon go back to the land of her childhood. Unfortunately, before this occurred, Matilda would go through a time of great peril.

The near tragedy for Matilda unfolded when Strong Loin's master informed his wife and son Mike that the family needed a buck or two and would need to sell a pig over at the Order Buyers in Galesburg. In due time, son Mike took a pig over to the Q Stockyards and sold it for a good price of $43.90. Arriving back home, he proudly showed the bill of sale to his mama. His mother suddenly became very pale and said in a weak voice, "Sonny, we don't have any pigs that weigh over 250 pounds. You have sold Matilda."

Immediately, the family attempted to get hold of Sammy Coffman at the Order Buyers, but he was not around. The hour was growing late, and soon the locomotives would be switching in the stock cars and Matilda would be on her way to the big city. While all of this was going on, Matilda became very uncomfortable and unhappy, as she was being crushed in a big pen with pigs that had never been pets. No one paid any attention to Matilda's squeals and protests.

Frantic appeals by the Grady family to members of the Order Buyers staff appeared to be to no avail, and everything seemed to be organized confusion. At the last moment, when Matilda was about to go to the sorting pen for shipment, Les of the Order Buyers staff had the fate of Matilda placed in his hands.

Les was heard to say by the folks in the office, "There are hundreds of hogs in the yards; how can I tell which one is Matilda?" A near miracle appeared to happen. To the rescue came seventeen-year-old Mike Grady, who exclaimed, "But Matilda is a pet pig, she will know her name. Let me go down there and say, Matilda come out, oh Matilda come out and she will come out."

The good news is that young Mike did ask Matilda to come out, and when she heard her name called a great happiness came over her. Disdainfully, Matilda pushed the other pigs aside and she indeed did come out. Matilda's hours of peril had passed and she accompanied Mike home to be reunited and live happily with Strong Loin and the Clyde Grady family on the farm that bordered on the lake known as Rice.

We are indebted to Mike Grady, a retired railroader from Knoxville, who saved Matilda and ensured a happy ending to the republishing of this neat story.

Leonard Woods pointed out in the ending of his original story that both you and the hogs will be much happier when you sell to the Galesburg Order Buyers, where the adult pigs are selling from $17.75 to $18.25.

Galesburg's Most Popular Bears

Galesburg has been blessed with a variety of parks since the turn of the century. The history of the Galesburg park system actually began in 1858, when Mayor Samuel Brown declared the need for a citywide system. A year later, little Standish Park sprouted from land currently next to the Knox County Courthouse.

In 1872, city fathers made a small effort to enhance the park system by planting thirty elms and maples in the center of the Public Square. In 1905, a city park committee purchased seventy-eight acres at $115 an acre from the Blue Farm north of Galesburg. The land would later become Lincoln Park, named after the former president.

In 1918, a direct bus line was established from downtown to Lincoln Park. The few fortunate enough to have autos didn't dare risk the treacherous roads that led to the park. Then, in 1919, a new craze swept the country—golf—and eventually a golf course was added to Lincoln Park.

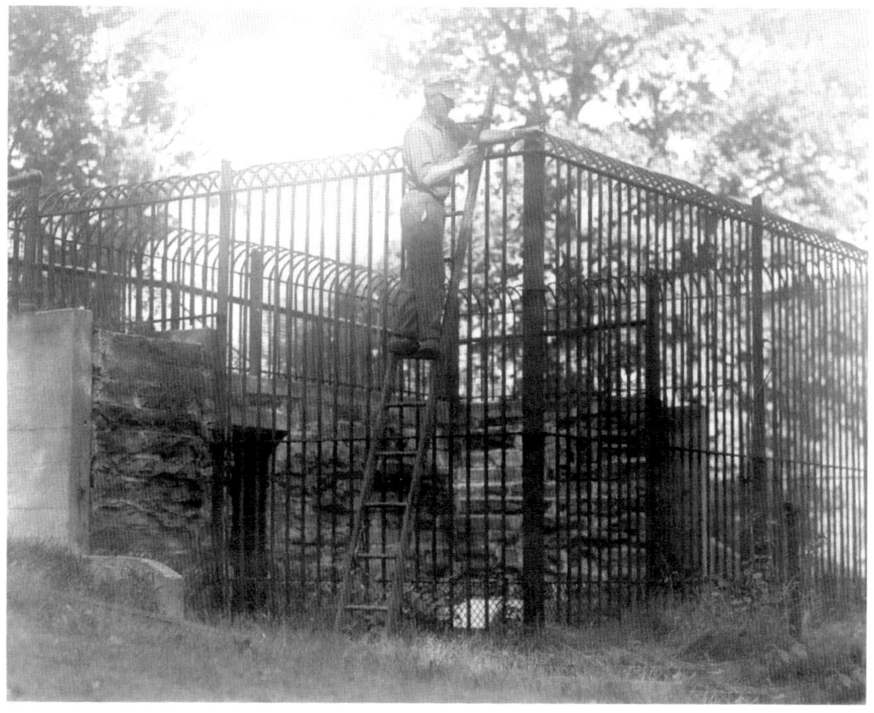

The Galesburg Lincoln Park Zoo bear cage.

Although Lincoln Park was taking shape in the early '20s, city officials realized more was needed. Mayor Henry Hawkinson, a great lover of youngsters, conceived an idea for a mini zoo to further enhance the park. City workers constructed a bandstand in 1925 for summer concerts and the Galesburg Lions Club installed a wading pool for little tots. An enclosed den with steel bars was constructed that would be home to two bear cubs that were initially bottle fed by John Olson, who single-handedly took care of Lincoln Park until the mid-'30s. On several occasions, the brown mama bears gave birth to tiny cubs. Smaller animals also were kept in the fenced area around the bear den. Long before television, talking movies and even Little League, people would flock to Lincoln Park to view the two bears. Although the bears were usually very tame, Olson was twice bitten in the hand while playing with the duo.

Olson would mow the entire park after walking each day from his home on North Cedar Street. Later, he was given the luxury of a horse to pull the mower around the vast park area.

As the bears matured in the early '30s, their dispositions deteriorated and it was decided, unfortunately, to discontinue the miniature park zoo. In 1942, by action of the Galesburg City Council, the scrap metal from the zoo fencing was donated to the war effort for the making of tanks, guns, ammunition and other materials. Eventually the iron cage that housed the popular bears was sold for a whopping $26.34, which was placed in the city's park department fund.

Most park-goers were content with the facilities at Lincoln; however, former Galesburg mayor William O.R. Bradley said in 1913, "A park without a lake is like a meal without salt." Galesburg was fortunate that in 1930 Santa Fe Railroad president W.B. Storey developed Mayor Bradley's idea and secured land west of Lincoln Park for its lake to provide water for steam locomotives. The lake eventually was turned over to the city and the rest is history.

Activity at Lincoln Park slowed slightly with the addition of Lake Storey, but Lincoln Park can't escape its fame as the park from which most others sprouted.

GALESBURG BEARS ESCAPE

In the 1920s, area residents enjoyed viewing the two bear cubs at the mini Lincoln Park Zoo north of Galesburg. In mid-August 1921, Hal and Al, the popular bear cubs, decided that life in their zoo-type den was much too confining and decided to explore the park area and possibly venture into the city. After lumbering through the wire mesh by which they were surrounded, they advanced upon P.D. Duff's refreshment stand. Their adventures prompted a near riot and resulted in Galesburg Police and city officials being summoned to Lincoln Park.

No doubt, the shenanigans turned into a glorious occasion for Galesburg's favorite pets, Hal and Al. After upsetting everything they could place their paws on in Duff's Emporium, they uncovered a gallon jar of orangeade syrup and quickly consumed the contents. Greatly strengthened and stimulated by the beverage and receiving a "bear of a kick," the furry couple proceeded to present an exhibition of tree climbing throughout the park.

Soon Mayor Hawkinson and several city fathers arrived on the scene in hopes of restoring order. Hal and Al refused to cooperate with the city dads and continued to disport themselves in a highly undignified manner. The Lincoln Park goody commissioner decided enough was enough and came armed with marshmallows and candy. Cubby Hal fell for the peace offerings and submitted to capture.

Unfortunately, Cubby Al decided to make it a more adventures day and charged the park kitchen, where he started extensive exploration proceedings. Mrs. Earl Bridge and Mrs. E.E. Hinchliff, who were enjoying an outing at Lincoln Park with their children, came to the rescue and locked Cubby Al in the kitchen. Enter Alderman "Husky" Johnson and Joe Anderson, who were acting as consultants on the case. They hit upon a brilliant idea to bring Hal back to the scene of his brother's depredations, which proved successful in coaxing his relative back safely to their lair.

It should be noted that Alderman Max J. Mack, when urged to join the expeditionary forces, stated that although present, he was not voting in this instance. Mack said that he had implicit confidence in the ability of his fellow councilmen and the mayor to take care of matters and any contributions on his part would be decidedly out of order. In all fairness to Mr. Mack, he was personally acquainted with Hal and Al. He had assisted in bringing the woolly bears from Avon to Galesburg originally. Mack considered himself close friends with the pair, even though Hal had taken a less than friendly smack at the city leader during the trip from Avon that ended in Lincoln Park.

Pooch Captured by Prisoners of War

One of the most remarkable construction projects ever staged in Galesburg occurred in the mid-1940s with the building of Mayo General Hospital. It was confirmed in early 1943 that Galesburg would be the site of an expansive hospital facility to treat and rehabilitate wounded World War II veterans.

Located just outside the northern border of Galesburg off Seminary Street, the $5 million project grew out of 156 acres of farmland owned by the Deets and Setterdahl families. When completed in under nine months, it included 118 brick buildings with one and a half miles of connecting corridors. Considered a city within a city, it included a chapel, theatre, gymnasium, indoor swimming pool, post exchange, tailor shop, barber and beauty shops, telegraph office, library, laundry and postal substation.

Over 19,000 wounded and ill patients received treatment in the 3,000-bed hospital. Due to the one-story construction, many paraplegic patients were treated. The staff included 134 officers, 136 nurses, 165 Women's Army Corps members, 686 enlisted men, 19 Red Cross workers and 800 civilian employees.

Several previous readers of the "Tracking History" column have inquired if there really was a German prisoner of war camp as part of the facility. Yes, during April 1945 approximately 160 German POWs reportedly captured in the Africa campaign arrived on site. They were housed in four wire-enclosed wooden barracks, located in the northeast quadrant. The POW section contained a mess hall and recreation room. The prisoners were used to supplement labor for Mayo General Hospital and available work throughout the area. At one time, prisoners from the Galesburg facility joined those incarnated at nearby Camp Ellis to harvest the pumpkin crop at Morton, Illinois. They also planted over nine hundred trees and bushes, many of which are still growing on the Hawthorne grounds today.

A very neat story involving the life of a seven-year-old Galesburg boy and his pet dog has come to light. Jerry Anderson and his parents lived on North Kellogg Street. One morning young Jerry woke to find that his brown and white mixed breed beagle pup was missing. After several days of unsuccessful searching, it appeared that Jerry's pal Sarge would not return.

Now to the rest of the story! It should be noted that Jerry's mother, grandparents and aunts were employed at Mayo General Hospital. His mother Veneta, grandmother Gladys, aunt Carol McMeen and aunt Twyla Diehl worked in the Mayo PX. His grandfather Art McMeen was the guard at the main gate located at Seminary and Walsh Streets, the current site of the Watson Funeral Home.

It came to light later that grandpa Art spotted the wayward dog Sarge roaming around the German POW camp. The prisoners begged Art to allow them to adopt the dog. Art displayed great compassion and felt that Sarge would help the prisoners' morale. Grandpa Art's compassion for the

German POWs appeared to highlight the local attitude about America's concern for the well-being of foreign war prisoners.

About six months later, a decision was made to abandon the Mayo Hospital German POW camp and ship the prisoners out of Galesburg. Speculation was that Sarge the dog would probably go along with the POWs; however, this was not the case. Apparently the German prisoners had compassion for Sarge and turned him loose.

Yes, the story has a very happy ending. Sarge left the Mayo Hospital grounds, much to the astonishment of Grandpa Art, and found his way home to his master Jerry. It was apparent that Sarge had received excellent treatment from his temporary friends, as he had gained over ten pounds. Jerry Anderson, retired after twenty-six years with the Galesburg Fire Department, reported happily that Sarge remained with the Anderson family for many years thereafter.

This is just one of the remarkable stories revolving around the complex that today is known as the Hawthorne Center.

CHAPTER 8

THE BURG IS INVENTIVE

DANDELIONS ON YOUR LAWN

In 1837, twenty-five members of the Silvanus Ferris family headed west from New York and were among the earliest settlers of Galesburg, Illinois. Eventually the family more than doubled in number. The exploits and adventures of the Ferris family were indeed a who's who in the history of Galesburg. Among the six adventurous sons of Silvanus was Olmsted Nathan Ferris.

Olmsted Ferris was best described as a true Jack of all trades in the early Galesburg community. He operated the first sawmill, was a dairyman, introduced sheep to the area and raised over sixty acres of popping corn. Olmsted was best known for introducing the popular American delicacy of popcorn to England. He took twenty barrels of popcorn and a load of fine cattle to London and popped his product before the eyes of astonished Britishers. This led to his being invited to Windsor Castle to pop corn for Queen Victoria. A former Galesburg resident, Emily Arnold McCully, produced a children's book on the subject entitled *Popcorn at the Palace*, which is available at the Galesburg Public Library.

Olmsted Nathan Ferris one-upped himself before his departure from England. While scouring the countryside, he came across a bright yellow plant growing in country gardens and along the highways. Upon inquiry, he was told that the beautiful specimen, called dandelion, had several culinary and medicinal uses. The dandelion was grown in England as a leaf vegetable and used to make wine. Olmsted was so impressed that he secured a quantity of the seed and brought it home to America.

Upon Olmsted's return to America, he dropped off samples of the dandelion seed to relatives in New York and Ohio. The balance of the seed was brought back to his farm west of Galesburg, scattered in his garden and cultivated as both a flower and vegetable. Although the dandelion was a novelty at first, Galesburg residents woke up to the fact that the bright yellow plant did not have to be cultivated and would grow anywhere at the least provocation. The seed was carried by the winds to the four corners of the earth and grew wherever it lodged.

Ferris family members pointed out that Olmsted did not live to fully realize the effect of bringing the dandelion seed here. It was evident that the immediate Ferris family clan often regretted his gift to America after realizing what a pest and nuisance it became.

Olmsted Ferris and his wife Currence had nine children, including William, who founded the city of Riverside, California. William was affectionately known as "Uncle Billy" and farmed on a ten-acre lot across from Hope Cemetery. William was Galesburg's first milkman and iceman, and he introduced both the wine press and ice cream to the area. It is interesting to note that Uncle Billy's Bakery on South Seminary Street was named in honor of William Ferris

Despite the multitude of activities engaged in by Olmsted Ferris, he became antsy and joined the famous forty-niners in their quest to discover gold in California. Olmsted died in California from complications after being kicked by a horse in 1850. Although he was buried in California, friends erected a monument in his memory at Hope Cemetery in Galesburg.

In case you were curious, the inventor of the famed Ferris wheel, George W. Ferris, was a nephew of Olmsted. The next time you are compelled to go out to the front lawn with a dull case knife and spend backbreaking hours eradicating the dandelion, you can thank Olmsted Ferris, who was one of ours.

AUTOMOBILE MADE HERE

George Washington Gale Ferris, born in Galesburg during 1859, is credited with designing and building the famous Ferris wheel. Riley Root of Galesburg is credited with inventing the original railroad snow plow in 1855, although unfortunately he failed to register a patent.

Thanks to the ingenuity of Adolph Lincoln Nelson, who resided in Galesburg, this community produced both the Illinois and Gale motorcars. Nelson was born in Oneida, Illinois, in 1888 and was reared in Galesburg. In 1908, Nelson designed the Illinois automobile. In fact, with the aid of a local patternmaker and blacksmith, he was the entire assembly line. The three

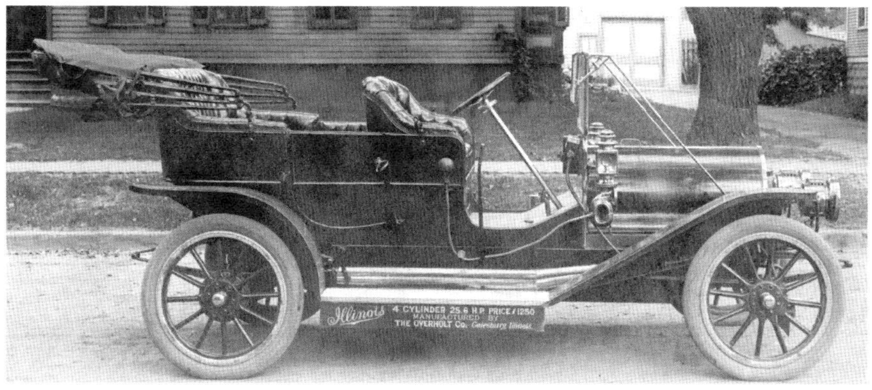

Illinois automobile manufactured in Galesburg, 1911.

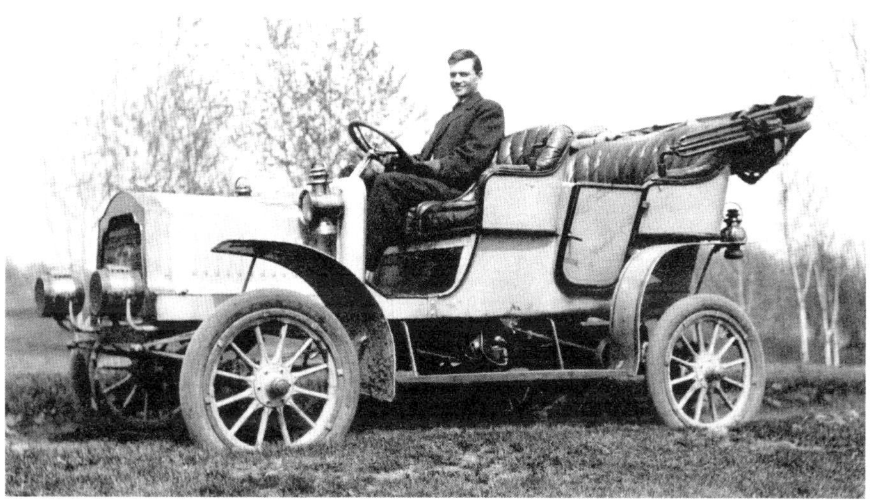

Gale automobile manufactured in Galesburg, 1907.

men made everything except the differential of the rear axle and the body. They produced a two-cylinder, air-cooled engine. Nelson did all the drafting of designs for the various parts. Nelson and his colleagues made the axles, friction drive transmission, hood, fenders, wheel spokes, rims and hubcaps.

The engine was in front under the hood; the piston-drive transmission was under the front seat, with a roller-type chain drive to the rear axle. Wheels on the Illinois car were small compared to the buggy-type on many cars of the time, and these had solid rubber tires. It took hand cranking to start the motor.

Cars produced in that time period needed to negotiate the mud roads to be practicable machines. Nelson frequently made road trips to both Peoria and Rock Island to test the vehicles' endurance under rough road conditions. Before starting on the trips, he often concurred with Walter Martin, owner of the Martin Motor Company in Galesburg, and Fred Peterson of the P&M Company.

Nelson continued to make improvements to the Illinois auto in 1909 and 1910. The later models included extras that allowed the buyer to purchase, for a small fee, both windshield and car tops. It appears that the original open models were the forerunner of sports cars driven today.

Without electric generators, the Illinois automobile, as was the case with other models of the day, had to produce power for headlights in other ways. Nelson used water gas, which shot a flickering light only a few rods in front of the car. The bodies of the vehicle were made of wood and steel.

Lincoln Nelson would eventually move his trade to Detroit, Michigan, and become prominently known for his superb designs of pistons for gasoline motors. Nelson proved himself quite remarkable during World War I by inventing the synchronized machine gun, which was timed so intricately that it shot its round of bullets through revolving airplane propellers.

Adolph Lincoln Nelson of Oneida and Galesburg most significantly left his trademark on early automobile manufacturing nationwide.

MOTHER BERG OR BURG?

In the early 1860s, Emma Halldahl Berg came to America following her marriage to Carl John Berg in Sweden. When still a small girl in Sweden, Emma began making a medical preparation that eventually would benefit people throughout the United States.

Beginning in 1863, Emma Berg began producing Mother Burg Salve from her residence at 243 North Pearl Street in Galesburg. The dark, heavy drawing salve was touted as a remedy for splinters, blisters, burns or whatever ailed you. The special formula salve was considered "Galesburg's Oldest Product." The claim was that people would use it to cure almost anything under the sun.

Mother Berg originally made two salves: the regular was dark brown and the lighter texture was considered the extra-strength one. The ingredients listed on an early tin included lard and beeswax. Speculation ran rampant as to the origin of the actual materials included in the popular salve. Many local residents actually thought that Mother Berg grew the ingredients in her garden. Others believe that most of the product came from Asia.

The Bergs had five children, including a daughter, Augusta, who changed the spelling of the family name to Burg. Emma's fame grew nationwide until her death at age sixty-eight in 1919. Augusta resumed making and marketing the salve upon her mother's death. Her husband, Charles J. Benson, was a local carpenter who passed away at age seventy-eight in 1944. At that point Florence Benson Carlson, granddaughter of Mother Berg, carried on the tradition.

It was not until 1958 that Harry E. Carlson, Florence's husband, made a decision to quit his railroad job and market the salve full time. The listing read, "Mother Burg Salve—Galesburg's Oldest Product." Mail orders came in from across the nation, many merely addressed only to "M.B.—Galesburg, Illinois."

Rumors circulated that Pepto-Bismol makers offered the Carlson family thousands of dollars to buy the rights; however, no actual proof has surfaced. Friends of the couple doubt that the family would have turned down such an offer.

Local pharmacist Don Tune, who owned the North Side Drug Store, apparently purchased the last known supply of Mother Burg's Salve. Tune was attempting to replenish his stock when he discovered that Mrs. Carlson was very ill in the hospital. Tune purchased the remaining six dozen tins just before Florence's death.

Attempts were made to have a Peoria lab analyze the ingredients, but to no avail. A Peoria firm, Mericon Industries, sold the product for about a year but the popularity decreased rapidly. Speculation was that as the product changed hands, a valuable part of the ingredients was omitted.

Many area residents will probably be looking in their medicine cabinets and even in attic storage boxes for a tin of Mother Burg's Salve.

A question remains today whether the inscription on the original containers read "Mother Berg" or "Mother Burg Salve."

Music Goes Round and Round

Many of us have hummed to the tune of "The Music Goes Round and Round." To jog your memory, here is the way it goes through the tooter horn:

I blow in here and the music goes down and round the corner…Wo ho ho ho…ho ho ho and it comes up here!
I push the first valve down and the music goes down and round…Wo ho ho ho and it comes up here!

I push the middle valve down and the music goes around below...below...
below...Deedle de ho ho ho!
I push the third valve down and the music goes down and round...Wo ho
ho ho...ho ho ho and it comes out here!

It appears that the words to this very popular song from the mid-'30s have a definite Galesburg connection. The words were penned by William Harold (Call Me Red) Hodgson, who performed regularly with the Ernie Palmquist Band from Galesburg. Ernie Palmquist and his band remain a mystery, and local band historians have been unable to shed light on them.

Maxine Smith, a reporter for the *Chicago American* newspaper, visited Galesburg during January 1936 to interview Red Hodgson and learn the true facts about his popular song. During the interview at a local skating rink, Red Hodgson asserted that he indeed wrote the words to the popular, goofy and insane song. It should be noted that several sites on the Internet credit Hodgson with writing the words and Ed Farley and Mike Reilley with writing the music. The Tommy Dorsey Orchestra played the tune extensively during the mid-'30s. The song was high on the Hit Parade List during the same time period.

Red indicated that he made the song up on a fluke in 1932 when he was playing trumpet and mellophone with the Ernie Palmquist Band in Galesburg. He decided to sing a song about his mellophone, so he began making up words as he sang. Red described the instrument as a curled-up tooter that looks like a French horn or a blown-up snail.

Maxine Smith discovered that Red Hodgson was only twenty-three years old when he penned the popular song. She described Hodgson as being tall and slim, with light red slick hair and a red mustache. He attended Penn State University following graduation from high school in Franklin, Pennsylvania. His father was a contractor.

So the next time you hum the popular, goofy and possibly insane tune "The Music Goes Round and Round," thank Harold Red Hodgson, a former Galesburg resident, for the memories.

MONUMENT FOR MOTHER

The Illinois General Assembly, meeting in Springfield on May 15, 1903, deemed it appropriate to furnish an unprecedented $5,000 for the erection of a suitable memorial to the memory of one of Galesburg's "Finest Ladies."

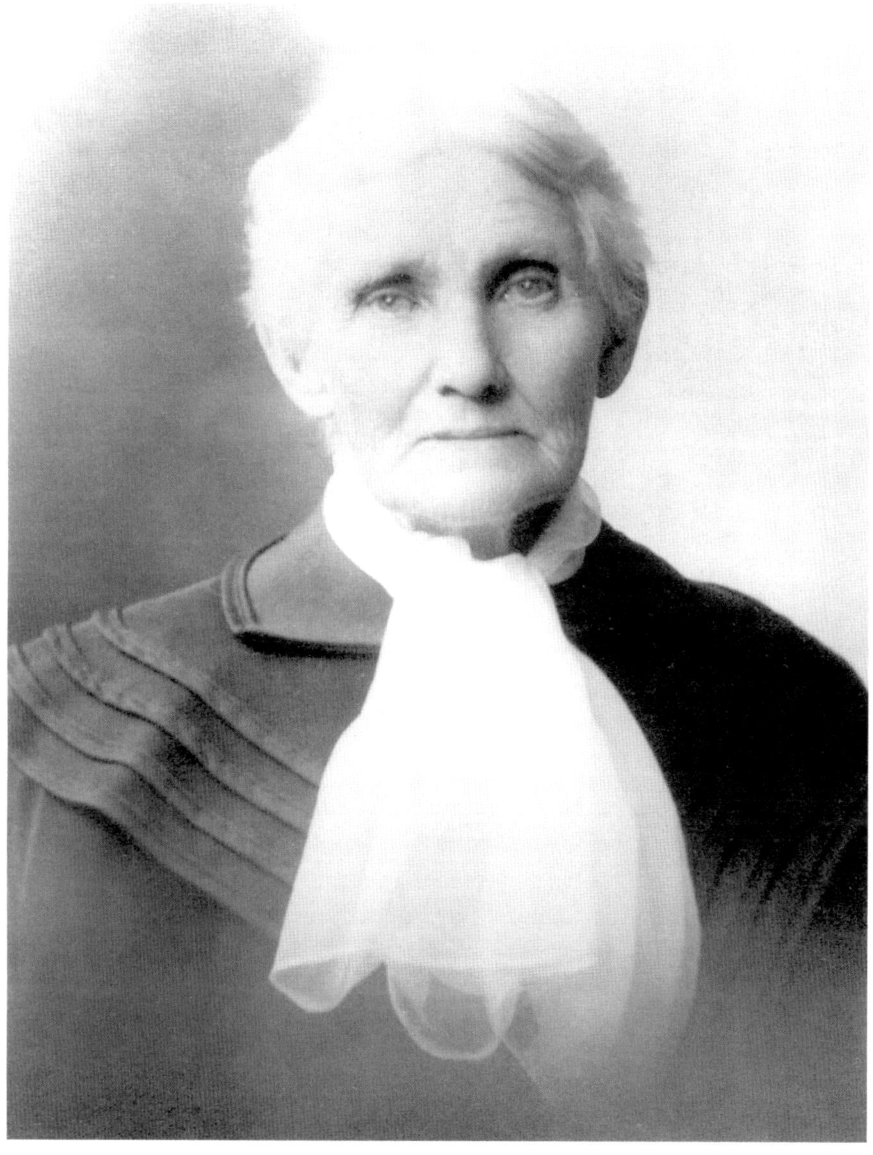

Mary Ann "Mother" Bickerdyke, famous Civil War nurse who was born in Galesburg.

The fine gesture by the Illinois General Assembly was in appreciation of the loving care of Civil War soldiers by a Galesburg, Illinois nurse named "Mother Bickerdyke." The appropriation of the monies further directed that the Mother Bickerdyke Memorial Association would have charge and direction of the erection of such memorial.

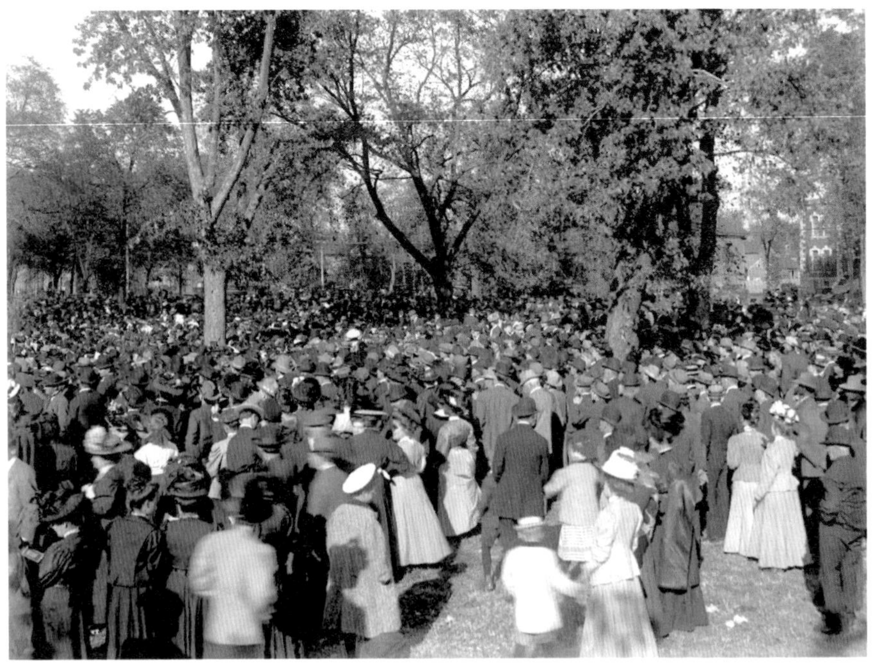

Bickerdyke statue dedication, showing hundreds of citizens in attendance, 1906.

The handsome Bickerdyke memorial was dedicated on May 22, 1906, on the northern lawn of the Knox County Courthouse. Over eight thousand area residents were present for the ceremonies, which commenced at 4:00 p.m. and lasted for over two hours. Speakers included former Illinois governor Richard Yates, Commander in Chief James Tanner of Washington, D.C., Galesburg mayor Lake W. Sanborn and relatives of Mother Bickerdyke. Mrs. Blazer James Rebstock, a member of the Knox County Board of Supervisors from Gilson, accepted the monument on behalf of the county. Also sitting on the platform was the sculptress, Mrs. Theo. A. Ruggles Kitson of Boston, Massachusetts.

Mrs. Fannie A. Blazer, president of the Mother Bickerdyke Memorial Association, said in her presentation, "Today we meet to commemorate the heroic deeds of a woman. It has been said of Abraham Lincoln that he was God's great gift to the American people. If that be true, surely Mother Bickerdyke was God's gift to the Union soldier. Galesburg has been honored to have her as a citizen."

The movement connected with the Bickerdyke monument spanned a period of five years. The first meeting was held on December 5, 1901, at the home of Mrs. Miron Rhodes. Mrs. Jennie Martin, the president of the Women's Relief Corps (WRC), appointed a committee to study the

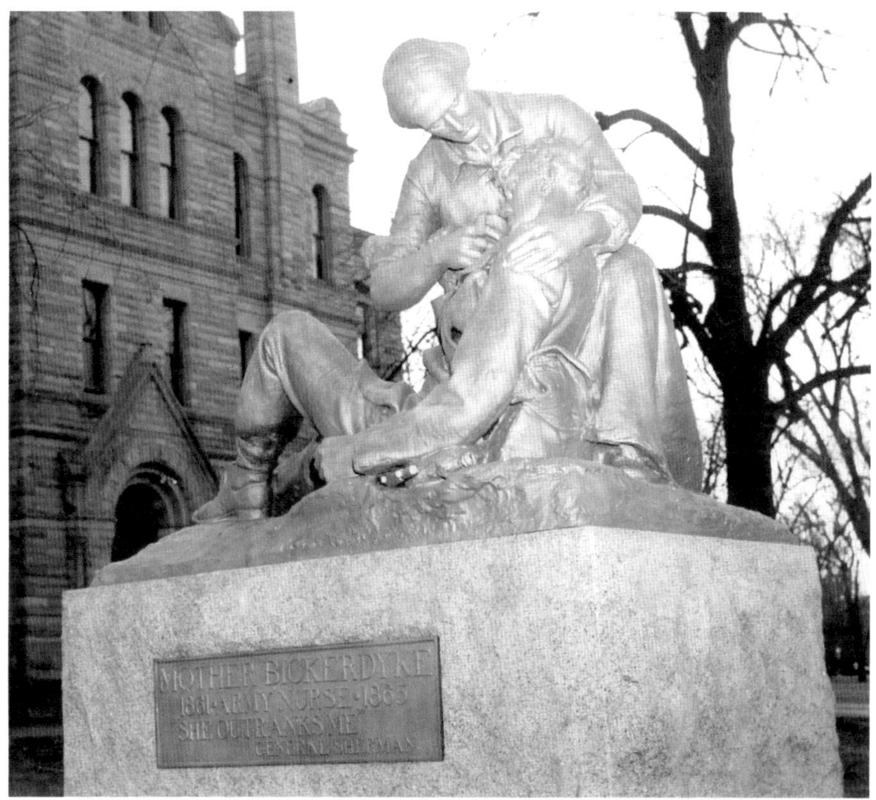

The Bickerdyke statue is located on the grounds of the Knox County Courthouse in Galesburg.

issue. The association initially sent out circulars to every post and corps in the United States in hopes of receiving contributions for construction of an appropriate monument. Mrs. Marietta Ervin had the honor of giving the first $25 toward the fund. Only $300 was collected, and it was feared that the amount needed would never be secured. This led the association to plead for financial help from the Illinois legislature. The original $300 in contributions were used to erect a monument at the grave of Mother Bickerdyke in Linwood Cemetery.

In 1943, an attempt was made by members of the Western Chroniclers, a local historical society, to name the planned new federal veterans' hospital on the north end of Galesburg after Mother Bickerdyke. The futile effort was spearheaded by Mrs. Ann Elphick, who resided on West Brooks Street. This was the same person who had attempted to relocate the Stephen Douglas burial plot from Chicago to Oquawka.

It is interesting to note that Mary Ann Ball was born in Knox County, Ohio, in 1817. In 1847, she married Robert Bickerdyke of Cincinnati, Ohio, and the couple moved to Galesburg, also in Knox County, with their children in 1856. Mary Ann "Mother" Bickerdyke passed away in 1901 and is buried in a plot at Linwood Cemetery alongside her husband.

During October 1958 brief services were held at the courthouse lawn monument to honor Mother Bickerdyke by the Illinois State Historical Society. Alexander Summers, president of the society, spoke, along with Reverend Ernest Fisher, pastor of the Central Congregational Church. Nurses representing both Cottage and St. Mary's Hospitals were in attendance.

On May 12, 2007, rededication ceremonies were held at the recently restored Mother Bickerdyke Monument to honor one of Galesburg's "Truly Finest Ladies." Appropriately, members of the Knox County Board and alumni of the Galesburg Cottage Hospital Historical Committee participated in the historical ceremony.

CHAPTER 9

RIDING THE RAILS

ALL TRACKS LEAD TO GALESBURG

It has been 153 years since the Burlington Railroad dispatched its first train out of Galesburg. A few hundred shivering passengers rode flat cars on a round trip between Galesburg and Wataga. It was reported that the majority of riders were younger people who had accepted the invitation for the free inaugural ride.

The passenger train, drawn by the Reindeer, pulled away from the Mulberry Street crossing at 1:30 p.m. and three hours later, shortly before sundown, returned to Galesburg. At the time, the Burlington had a fleet of four locomotives. In addition to the Reindeer, there were the Roebuck, the Antelope and a switch engine called the Pigeon.

Few early residents could visualize the enormous effect the rail industry would have on Galesburg. In the initial days of railroading, the city had a population of only 1,400. In the early 1900s, the system grew to over six hundred miles of track in the Galesburg Division. Over 5,000 people were served daily at the passenger depot. The Galesburg Division operated the largest "Hump Switch Yards" in the nation and handled over fifteen thousand freight cars annually. Over 2,500 people received railroad employment, producing a payroll of more than $200,000 monthly.

By the mid-'20s, the Burlington Line was handling a freight train every fifteen minutes. The volume of traffic necessitated the construction of five additional tracks. A new state-of-the-art depot was constructed on South Seminary Street and a subway was built south of the facility that is still in use today. In 1943, CB&Q president Ralph Budd announced that Galesburg would become the main terminal point for the entire Burlington system.

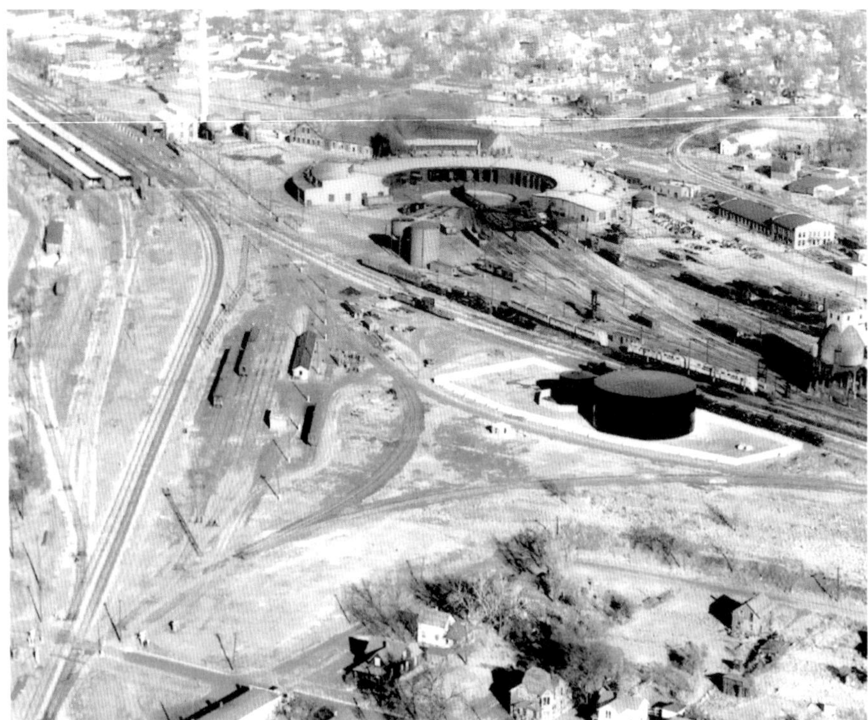

Aerial view of CB&Q rail yards and locomotive roundhouse in Galesburg, 1950. *Photo courtesy of William Frankey.*

In 1947, the national rail publication *Trains* highlighted the fact that tiny Galesburg had become the "major traffic center of the Chicago, Burlington and Quincy Railroad." The article pointed out that Galesburg was the stopping place for every one of the thirty-one passenger and forty freight trains that daily rolled over the six lines radiating to the east, west, north and south.

The Willis Yard south of Galesburg contained the largest individually owned railroad hump yard in the world. The tie-treating plant located between the city and Abingdon served the entire eleven thousand miles of the Burlington Railroad in fourteen states. *Trains* magazine highlighted the fact that the forty-one-stall roundhouse and huge turntable accommodated locomotives up to 125 feet in length.

In 1947, the average stay of a one-hundred-plus-car freight train was about two hours. Servicing and changing locomotives was done at the rate of three to five cars a minute. It was estimated that over six thousand freight cars rolled over the Galesburg humps for classification in every twenty-four-hour period.

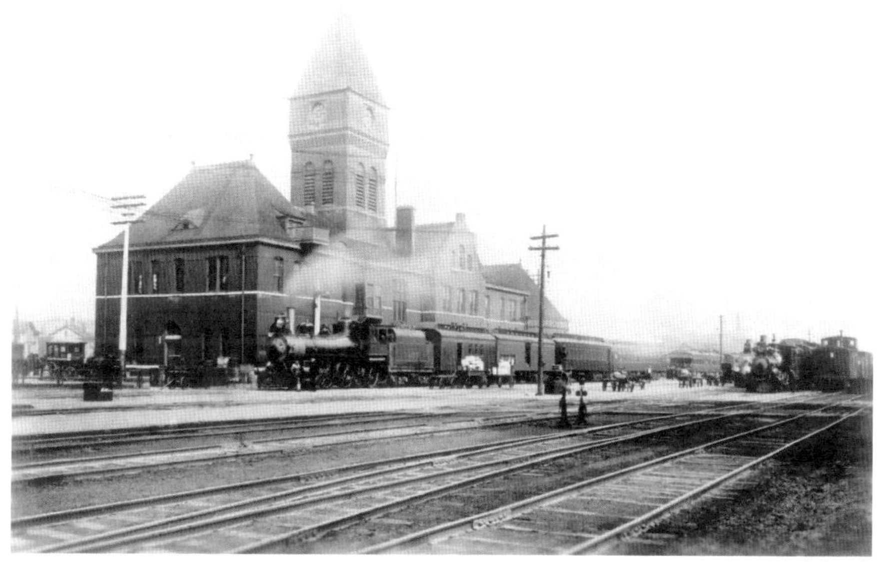

CB&Q Rail Depot and steam locomotive in Galesburg, 1900.

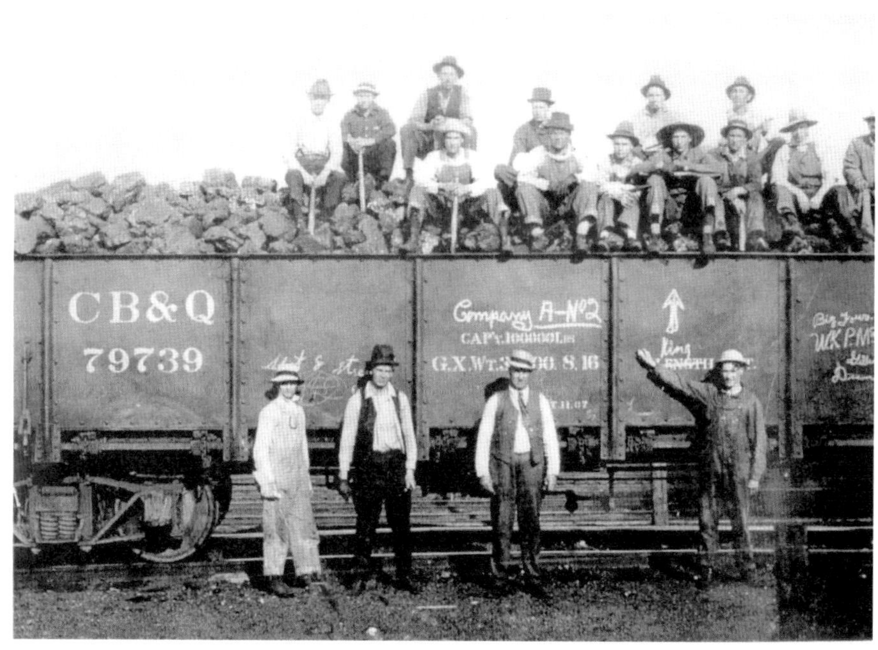

CB&Q coal car in Galesburg railroad yards, 1920. *Photo courtesy of William Frankey.*

Joseph Mills, who started as a conductor on the CB&Q Railroad in 1897, recalled the primitive methods used in early rail operations. Mills originally was a callboy who dashed to all parts of the city on a bicycle notifying train and engine crews to report for work. Mills reminisced that when he began, the engines had a long pilot bar on the front of the "cow catcher" used to couple cars together. The brakeman would rest the car on his knee and guide it into position with one hand and, with the second hand, drop in pins that locked the cars together. Mills pointed out, "If you missed, an undertaker had to wash your face and tie your tie."

Mills explained that freight cars had no air brakes and all braking was done by hand. Brakemen were paid $1.90 per hundred miles and usually worked up to sixteen hours daily. Mills illustrated that passenger conductors wore long-tailed coats, balloon pants and carried a long gold chain with a heavy gold watch attached. Several of the more flamboyant drove to the station for work in first-class surreys with matched teams of horses. The conductors were considered the aristocrats of railroading.

It is becoming increasingly apparent that the industry that formed Galesburg will likely preserve it.

TRAIN VANISHES DURING SNOWSTORM

One of the most interesting and unique forms of transportation in local history was the Fulton County Narrow-Gauge Railroad. The line extended from the west bank of the Illinois River for sixty-one miles from Havana to Galesburg. At first glance, the locomotive and passenger cars looked normal, but they were not; they were miniatures.

The rails were laid out only three feet apart, compared to the standard four feet, eight inches as used by the CB&Q Railroad. The rails twisted throughout the bottomlands, avoiding high places, and appeared to curve like a serpent from Galesburg to Havana. The line from Havana to Fairview opened in 1880 and the extension to Galesburg began in 1882. The line called the Peavine was conceived from a newspaper editor's dream during a struggle by Lewistown to retain the Fulton County seat that was being sought by Canton.

One of the most unique features of the Peavine line was its "real" personal service. The slim-gauge trains were known to wait for hours past departure time for a passenger's meeting to end. When a teachers' institute in Lewistown lasted longer than expected, the train's departure was delayed until the session closed.

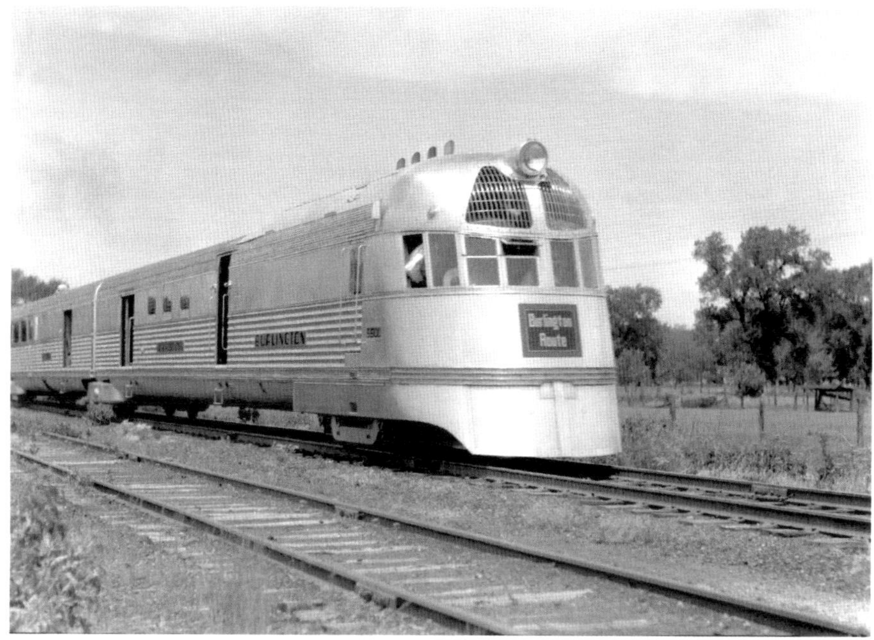

Burlington Railroad Zephyr on tracks in front of Galesburg depot.

It was not uncommon for the train to stop along the route through Ellisville at Coal Creek while passengers hopped off and fished for an hour or more. Old-timers passed on tales of conductor George Kessler carrying a high-powered rifle on his runs and shooting down wild game from the platform as the none-too-speedy Peavine chugged along the Spoon River.

It was not uncommon for farmers, hearing the distress whistle from the snowbound Peavine, to come to the rescue with shovels and clear the tracks of obstructing drifts. During one of those too frequent snowstorms, somehow, somewhere the train became lost for almost two days. The Peavine left Galesburg at 6:20 a.m. on Tuesday, February 8, 1885, and headed south toward Havana during a whopping blizzard. Galesburg train agent King Mathews thought the snow had abated sufficiently and sent the train on a near disastrous journey.

As the day dragged on, word came from London Mills that the train had failed to arrive. When negative reports continued into Wednesday morning, Mathews and a companion set out at 10:00 a.m. to find the train. Unbelievably, they trudged the icy track on foot. Along the way, the Galesburg ticket agent lost his overshoes in a snowdrift and the pair was forced to take temporary refuge in a farmhouse.

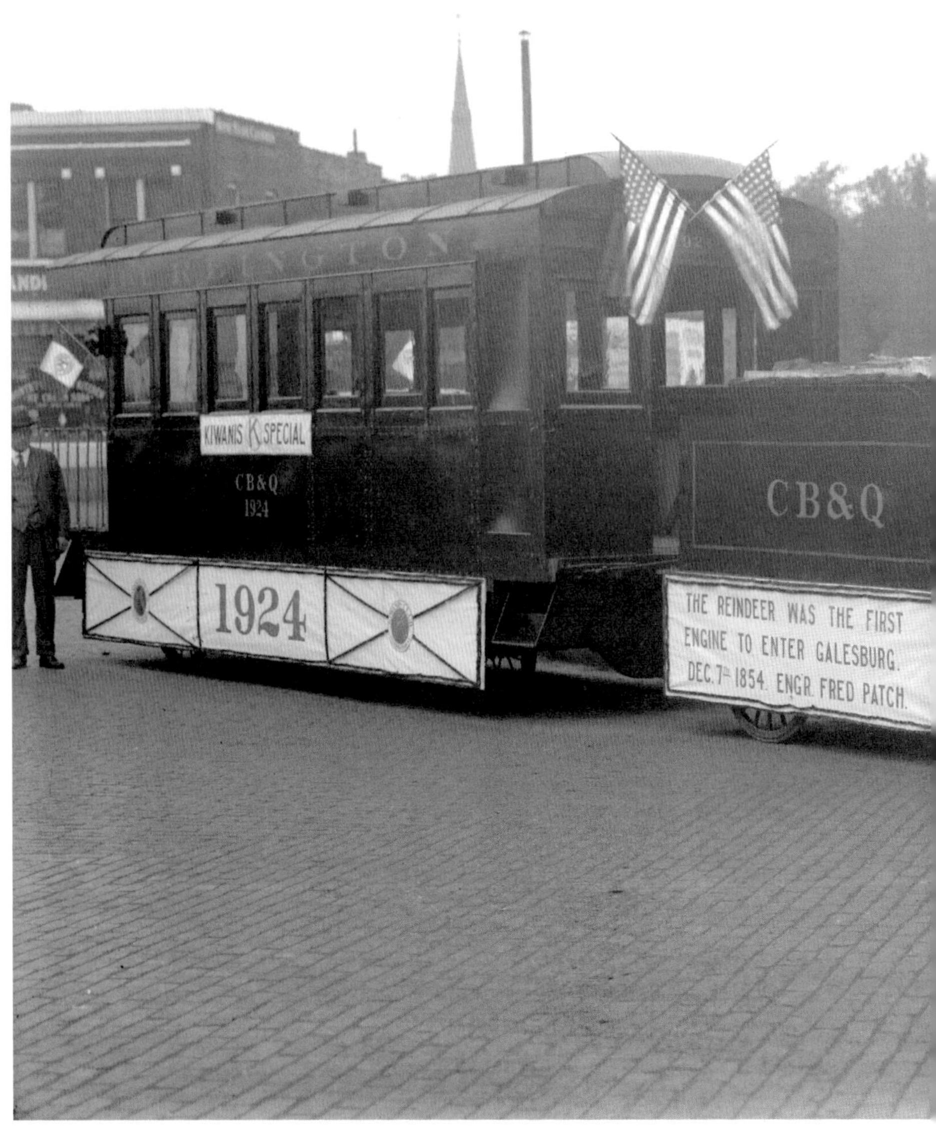

Replica of the original train, the Reindeer, that arrived in Galesburg on December 7, 1854.

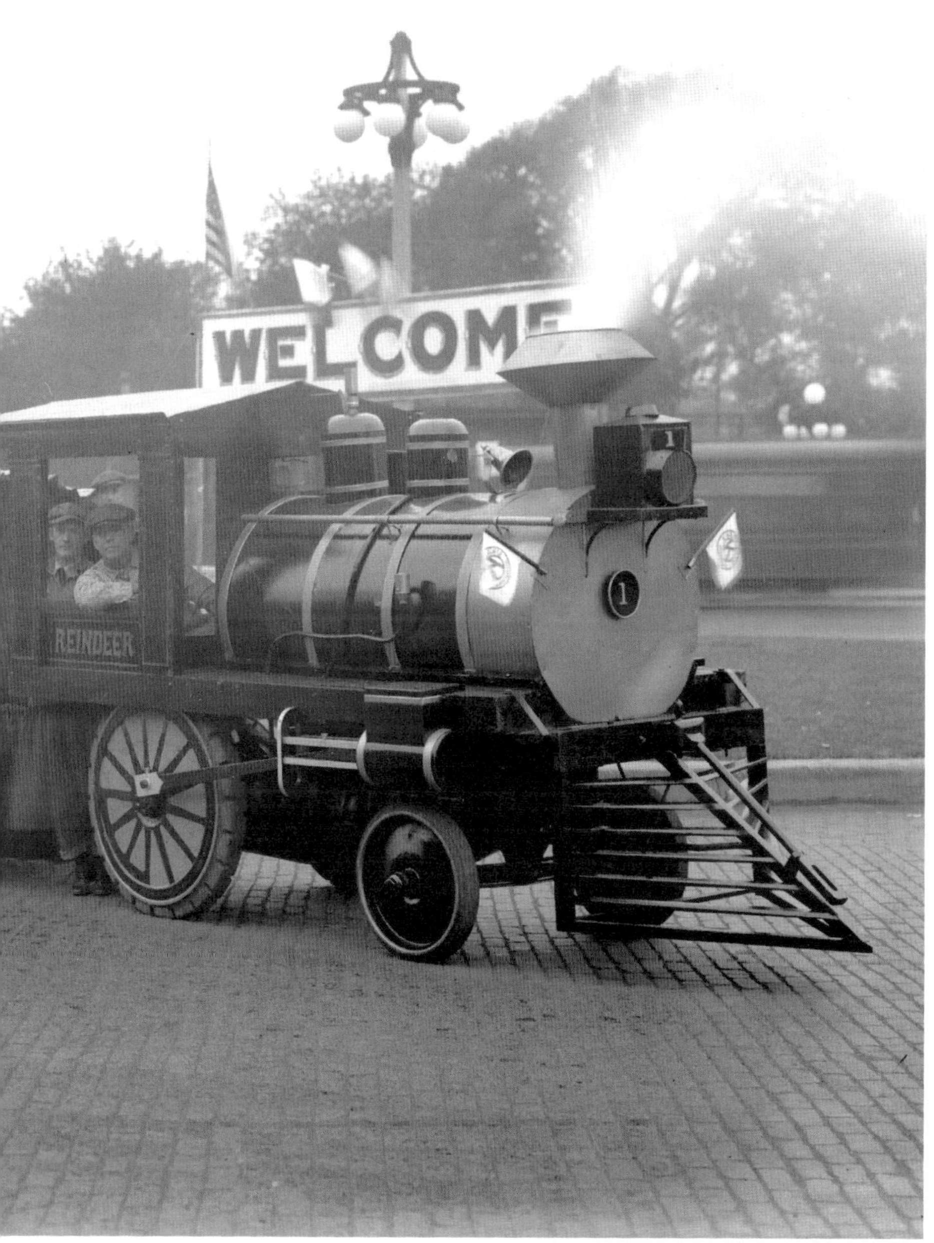
WELCOME
REINDEER

After completing the ten-mile hike to DeLong, they learned that the missing train was snowbound at Brush Creek. The crew and twelve passengers took turns staying awake and keeping a fire going in the passenger car overnight. All they had to eat was candy and crackers. They were finally able to escape to DeLong, but the train was delayed on the spot until Friday, four days following its original departure.

The honor roll of those who actually worked on the Knox and Fulton County Narrow-Gauge included Reuben Simms, Tink Grier, Charles Ekstrand, A.J. O'Donnal, Buddy Young, Charlie Eskridge, Ben Evans, Joe Day, William Dolph, Hugh Coole, Billy McCowan, John Mack, M.M. Clark, William Rosellan, J.J. McNally, W.T. Scott, W.B. Lloyd, A. Daugherty and Bryan Scanlan.

Interest in the Knox/Fulton County line has never died. It was aided when E.W. Mureen, a former mayor of Galesburg, wrote a book on the subject in 1943. It was unique that Mureen never worked on the railroad.

CHAPTER 10

FUN THINGS TO DO

Knox County Fair Oldest?

The Knox County Fair lays claim to being the "Oldest Existing Chartered Fair in Illinois." The Macoupin County Fair in Carlinville claims to be the oldest in Illinois, dating back to 1852. Although records are sketchy and possibly arguable, the Knox County Fair at its present location was chartered by the Illinois Department of Agriculture in 1851.

It appears that the first ever Illinois State Fair in Springfield was not held until 1853. Neither the streets of the capital nor the fairgrounds was paved and rains turned the grounds to a sea of mud. A newspaper reporter noted that there were more pigs on the streets of Springfield than at the fair. Springfield hosted the state fair again in 1854, but Alton, Centralia, Chicago, Decatur, DuQuoin, Freeport, Jacksonville, Olney, Ottawa, Peoria and Quincy played host prior to 1892.

Evidence exists that the first resemblances of a Knox County Fair likely began on the Public Square in Knoxville in 1839. Later, the fair was actually in the form of a gigantic picnic in a grove on the edge of Knoxville when it was the county seat. Farmers exhibited fruits and vegetables but no awards were given.

The 1937 fair resulted in the highest attendance and largest revenues up to that time. It was advertised as the eighty-first annual event and the largest, according to offered attractions. The midway featured the Zimdar Carnival, offering twelve rides and fourteen shows. Popular attractions included the Original WLS Barn Dance and an amateur talent contest that drew several dozen entries. Three days of harness races included entries from throughout the county. Bicycle races and running races featuring county farmers drew large attendance and much amusement. Instead of a tractor-pulling contest, a mule-pulling event proved popular.

Sammy Fox of Knoxville sang and whistled his way to the championship of the amateur contest. Unusual entertainment for a fair was provided in the form of a glee club contest. The Abingdon High School glee club won first place and a large gold loving cup. Wataga High School, represented by a trio of three girls, finished runner-up. Cummings School, taught by Helen Myers, was awarded the top prize for the best display of one-room schools.

Pre-fair advertising in 1937 highlighted the fact that all drives on the fairgrounds were cindered and admission was only $0.40 at the gate and $0.25 for the grandstand. Total attendance was a record 10,499 and ticket sales exceeded $5,000 for the first time in fair history.

The Knox County Fair has been held continually since its inception, with only two exceptions. Fair board members cancelled the 1862 event during the Civil War to allow the 102nd Regiment of Illinois Volunteers to use the grounds for its military camp. Directors voted not to hold a fair in 1942 because of the war.

One of the most unusual Knox County Fair racing events occurred in 1966, when radio personalities from WGIL and WAIK challenged one another to a race around the dirt track. The tension grew for days leading up to the much-anticipated race. Due to the fact that the world-famous Gene Holter's Movieland Wild Animal Show would be featured at the fair, it was decided that the local radio jocks would race while astride wild animals. Despite a steady rain and the fact that a hippopotamus ridden by WAIK news director Tom Wilson continually ran into the guardrail, the event thrilled a packed grandstand.

County fairs are such a popular attraction in Illinois that there are more fairs than there are counties. Illinois has 102 counties, but there are 105 fairs; 4 Illinois counties hold 2 events annually and 1, Livingston County, holds 3. Only 3 counties host no fair.

The 1958 Knox County Fair was billed as the 100th, which would make the 2009 event number 150—but who is actually counting?

BIG STORE MEMORIES

Remembrances of the former O.T. Johnson Big Store in downtown Galesburg continue to surface since the tragic fire that destroyed the building. In my lifetime I can't remember an event that has spurred so many memories.

When the O.T. Johnson Big Store closed its doors for good in 1978, neighbors in the 100 block of East Main Street disappeared one by one. The only one remaining currently is the Civic Art Center. Walgreen Drug Co.,

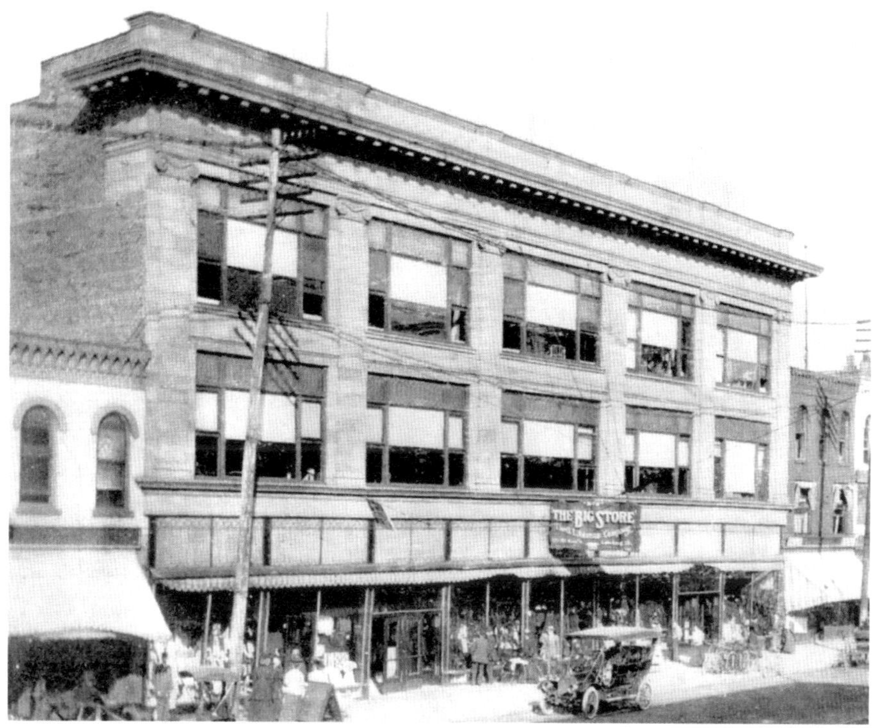

The O.T. Johnson Big Store in downtown Galesburg, 1926. The full-service department store was the largest in downstate Illinois at the time.

Allen's Appliance, the Continental Clothing Co. and Bergner's Department Store have relocated. Ross Shaver, Grothe Shoes, Halpern's Women's Wear and the Scandia Restaurant are also only memories.

It has also surfaced that the window decorator and sign painter employed at the O.T. Johnson Big Store in the early 1900s was a young man named Dick Blick. Mr. Blick would eventually open his own business in the Bondi Building that would become the nationally recognized Dick Blick Co.

A full-page ad in the *Galesburg Evening Mail* during November 1909 illustrated expansion of O.T.'s Main Street Big Store to the "Annex" to the north on Ferris Street. The furniture department stretched an entire block from Main to Ferris Streets on the third floor of each building. The overflow of furniture-related merchandise occupied the fifth floor of the Annex. The connecting buildings contained what was described as fourteen separate departments. The Big Store professed to be the most convenient possible, as it had broad aisles, high ceilings, the splendid Tungsten lighting system, easy stairways, two roomy elevators, comfortable toilet facilities, drinking fountains, free telephones and free parcel check rooms. It was in general a store for everybody.

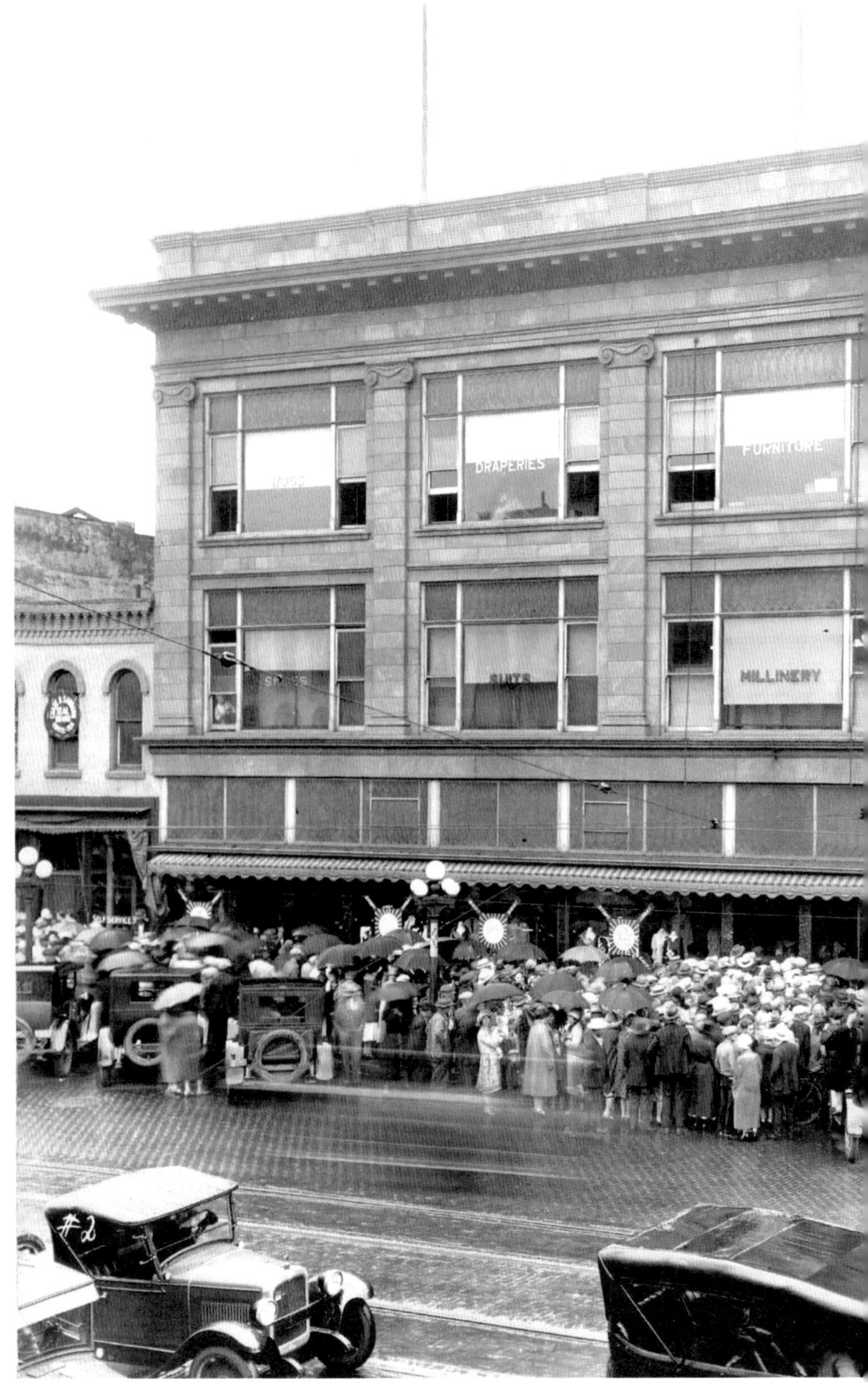

The O.T. Johnson Big Store in downtown Galesburg, 1920.

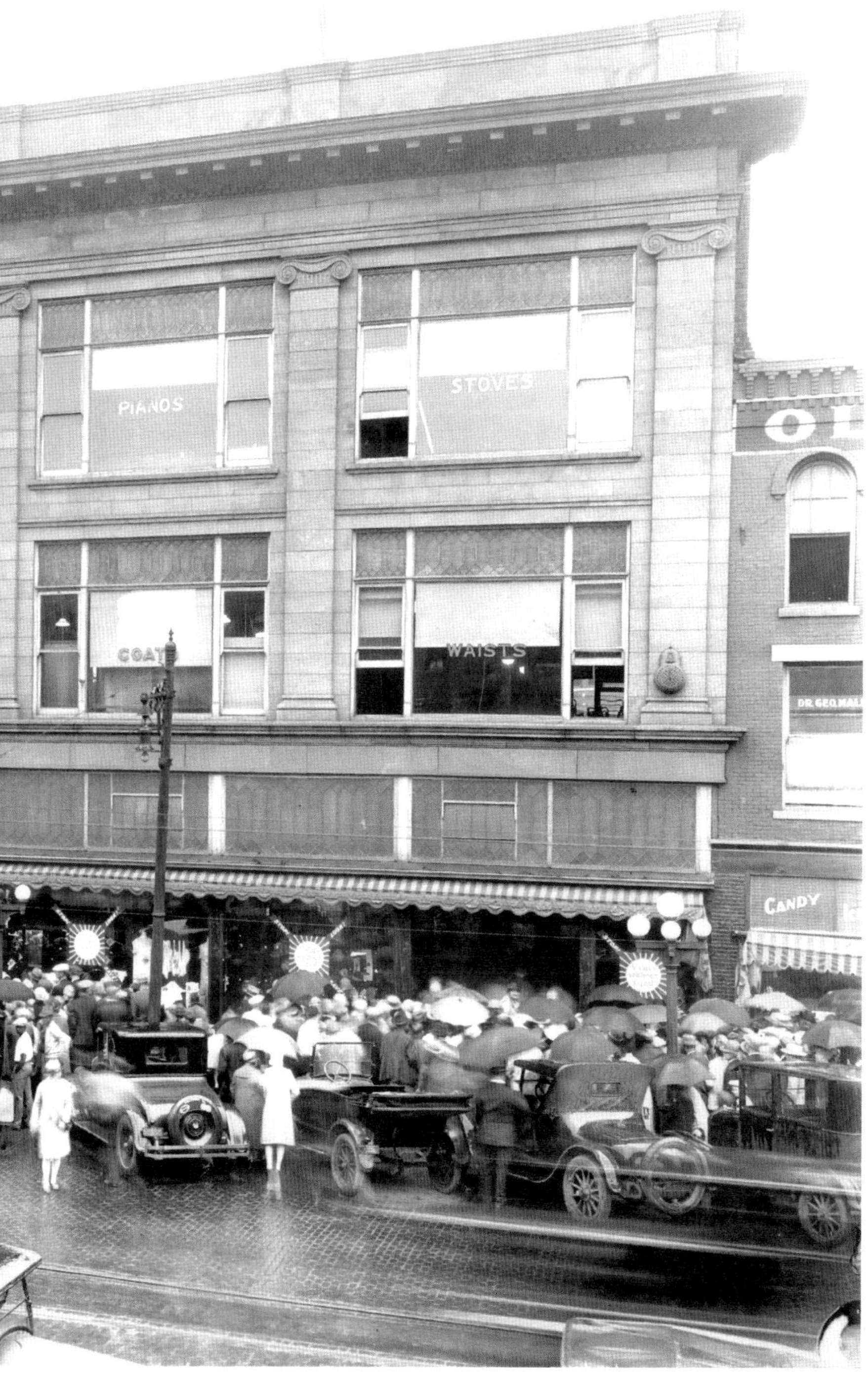
PIANOS
STOVES
WAISTS
CANDY

Old ledger books displayed in O.T.'s windows during the seventy-fifth anniversary in 1937 revealed that Galesburg shoppers were buying calico fabrics, coal oil, jugs of whiskey and hoops for hoop skirts when the store opened in 1862. Even in the beginning, the store strived to stock what customers wanted.

Prominent persons in the 1860s took advantage of O.T.'s convenient charge services. Some of the names appearing in the early charge ledgers included Judge Lawrence, James Cox, S.W. Irwin, L.V. Conger, P. Hawkinson, S.H. Ferris, Hank Sanderson, Minne Hatch and George Churchill. N.P. Nelson, who later entered business as a competitor, frequently appeared in the early charge accounts. O.T. Johnson occasionally delved into the cash drawer; however, he never failed to leave a charge slip against himself. On one page of charges appears purchases from the Angel family for thread and tatting. Mr. Hell is charged for coal oil and lamp chimneys. When a lady bought sewing supplies in the 1860s from O.T. Johnson, her husband was waiting on Main Street in the family hayrack to carry her back home.

The Big Store is unfortunately "no more"; however, the memories will surely linger forever.

ANNEXED BIG STORE

The fire at the former O.T. Johnson Annex warrants a history lesson on the facility. The addition enabled Galesburg to have the largest full department store in downstate Illinois.

O.T. Johnson came to Galesburg from Altona in 1860 and was employed by Sage and Reed. Two years later, he bought them out and launched the store bearing his name. He became a community leader and was elected Galesburg mayor in 1873. The fledgling Galesburg community prospered under Johnson's leadership.

In 1890, O.T. Johnson turned over operations of the Main Street store to Robert Chappell and moved to Riverside, California. His last appearance in Galesburg was during the O.T. Johnson store's fiftieth anniversary celebration in 1912.

In July 1909, Robert Chappell announced plans to more than double the floor space of the O.T. Johnson store. The sales floor space would increase from 60,000 to 125,000 square feet. The enlargement became necessary because of the ever-increasing flow that followed up-to-date methods of merchandising. The lot immediately to the rear of the Main Street facility, running a distance of 154 feet to Ferris Street, was chosen as the site for the five-story structure.

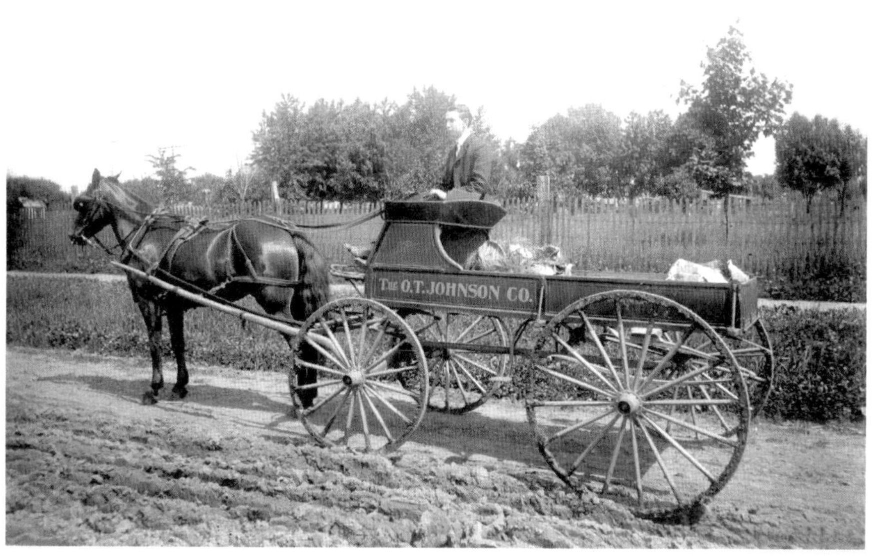

An O.T. Johnson Big Store horse-drawn delivery truck on a dirt road in Galesburg, 1880.

The building would be covered by Galesburg brick and steel exterior. The structure would include a full basement, at a total cost of $50,000. The ceilings were covered in metal, all windows were fireproof and a modern sprinkler system was installed throughout both buildings. A large wood and steel band water tower was installed on top of the new building to supply water for the sprinkler system. The water tower was taken down in 1988. Electric elevators were installed in both buildings.

J. Grant Beadle of Galesburg served as architect for the project. It was first thought that additional stories could be added to the Main Street store, as it was originally constructed for that purpose. A warehouse and a one-story brick house were razed to make room for the new structure.

Construction was hastened to accommodate much-needed space for furniture and carpeting. One floor of the Annex contained a large dining room that featured an oriental motif. When completed, the Big Store contained a camera shop, toys, an elaborate section of chinaware, lighting fixtures, paints, a soda fountain, a bakery, a flower shop, jewelry and an elaborate book and stationery section. Men's and women's fashions and a large shoe salon, which employed the father of future president Ronald Reagan, were considered the finest in the state.

What might have been a fire of large proportions was discovered in the Annex during construction. The lime house, which was located in the basement area, was discovered to be the seat of the fire. Several joists were badly burned and had to be replaced. Like the recent fire, prompt action by the Galesburg Fire Department kept the loss to a minimum.

For some undocumented reason, the Annex ceased being used for a sales area and was taken over by the Gross Uniform Company in 1929.

One of Galesburg's finest stores ever deserved the designation of the "Big Store."

A SCOOP OF ICE CREAM

With the exception of a column on Kiddieland, no other story has caused as much interest and confusion as Highlander's Ice Cream Stand. In one column, the location of the popular Highlander's was referred to as on Phillips Street. But most readers, and yours truly, remember the location as being 227 Arnold Street.

Where did yours truly ever come up with Phillips Street as the location where thousands of children and adults bought a huge cone brimming full of ice cream for a mere five cents? During August 1928, a Galesburg newspaper ran an interesting article describing the success of Highlander's. The bold headline read, "Thousand Cones Sold Each Day on Phillips St." As a recap, the article pointed out the fact that on a hot day, Highlander's manufactured up to 130 gallons of seven different varieties of ice cream a day. The article continued to refer to the location as Phillips Street. Phillips Street was and is located one block west of Arnold.

A reader of this column on the *Register-Mail* website from Vancouver, Washington, sent an e-mail concerning the exact location. This, of course, enhanced my curiosity and made me question my sanity. As a youngster, I grew up on both Division and Locust Streets and walked to Highlander's for a dip of ice cream a multitude of times. At this point it seemed appropriate to check Galesburg City Directories from that time period. This effort produced some interesting facts but did not answer the location question sufficiently.

From 1926 until 1938, the Galesburg City Directory listed Irvin and Florence Highlander as residing at 1560 East North Street, not on Arnold Street. It should be clarified that Irvin and Florence were the owners of the famous ice cream palace. Beginning in 1938, the Highlanders moved to 82 Madison and began manufacturing ice cream at that location. Finally, in 1941, the city directory listed 227 Arnold as their residence. It was apparent that Irvin did manufacture ice cream in a garage at the rear of 227 Arnold Street. We can assume that the location became the site of the ice cream stand and selling point. The 1944 Galesburg phone book listed the phone numbers for their residence at 227 Arnold as #5114 Brown and the ice cream stand as #5114 Blue. How many remember when a color was part of phone numbers?

Also in 1944, a nephew of the ice cream entrepreneurs, Clark Highlander, was an outstanding Silver Streak basketball player. Clark entered the navy upon graduation from Galesburg High School and later graduated from Purdue University. Clark would eventually be elected mayor of Flat Rock, North Carolina. This meant that both Clark and Carl Sandburg would migrate to the same city. During Clark's tenure as mayor, Flat Rock would become a sister city of Galesburg. In an attempt to solve the beginning location of Highlander's Ice Cream, yours truly called Clark, now residing in Columbus, North Carolina.

I learned that Clark scooped ice cream at the Arnold Street location during his high school years. His usual work schedule was from 5:00 to 10:00 p.m. seven days per week. He shared with me that he loved eating all of the flavors and would often mix them together to frustrate his uncle. Clark was not sure, but he thought it was possible that the initial location might not have been on Arnold Street, as his aunt and uncle did not reside there. For the record, the early residents of 227 Arnold were Ted and Hilma Lind. Clark verified that the Linds were related to the Highlanders.

For sure, the delicious Highlander's ice cream cone was sold from a gray portable ice cream stand located at 227 Arnold Street in the eastern section of Galesburg. What we still don't know for sure is whether Highlander's was originally located on Phillips Street. Maybe a reporter in 1928 drove a newspaper editor crazy by not typing the correct street name. It has been proven countless times that the best source of solving this mystery will surely come from interested readers.

And finally, were you aware that William Meade Ferris, formerly of Galesburg, has been credited with introducing ice cream to Illinois?

Magic in Monmouth

William Nicola was known in Monmouth during the late 1800s as an accomplished photographer. Photography was his vocation; however, magic was his prized hobby. He would soon become known as the "Great Nicola," one of the world's most renowned magicians.

William Nicola was born in Burlington, Iowa, on December 4, 1882, to John and Lettie Nicola. His father was a native of Scotland. It was no accident that William Nicola acquired his original vocation and hobby, as his father John was a leading photographer in the Maple City. His father took up magic at an early age and presented amazing shows throughout the Midwest.

Known to his friends as Will, the young Nicola began acting as his father's assistant at the age of six and made his first solo appearance doing small tricks at the Omaha Exposition to help attract crowds to McDonald's "Battle of Manila Show."

In 1900, while only eight years old, Will made his first European magic tour, working his way from Monmouth to Paris for an exposition in the French capital. While in Paris, he met Loie Fuller, who was also a native of Monmouth. Miss Fuller had gained fame nationally as a serpentine fire dancer. She agreed to sponsor Will while performing in Europe and he immediately became famous.

Nicola's initial appearance with a complete show occurred during February 1901, in the old Pattee Opera House in Monmouth. Will then became officially known as the "The Great Nicola" and appeared in shows in Chicago. As his success grew he performed in every state in the union, Canada and conducted five world tours, which consumed about three years each.

The Great Nicola became known as one of the greatest showmen of his time. He has been compared with great artists Thurston, Blackstone and even Houdini. He was billed as "the strangest man in the world." Each time Will returned from his foreign engagements, he would spend three months of the year in Monmouth perfecting new tricks and spectacles.

His last worldwide tour nearly ended in disaster. After playing in the Orient, he loaded his eighty tons of equipment on the British boat *Sirdhana* and, along with his fourteen-member troupe, sailed for a return to Monmouth. On November 13, 1938, the *Sirdhana* struck a British minefield off the shore of Singapore. Fifty lives were lost and the *Sirdhana* quickly sank, taking over $100,000 of Nicola's equipment and one-of-a-kind illusions to the bottom of the ocean. Miraculously, Will and his troupe, including his wife Marian, who grew up in Aledo, all survived. His business manager, Charles Hugo of Chicago, survived, along with his wife Josephine, who was the sister of "Fibber McGee" of radio fame.

Monmouth's Great Nicola was not only a great magician but an accomplished escape artist as well. He would hang suspended in a straitjacket, head down, from a rope attached to a multiple-story building, with his hands handcuffed behind him, and free himself within thirty seconds. Once he was placed in a county jail behind four locked steel doors and in a matter of minutes he was out.

When he first appeared in China, there was no place to perform, so he had five hundred Chinese workmen build a theatre in only five days. It was made of bamboo, didn't have a single nail and seated over three thousand. Part of Will's company was an elephant called Nizie whom he could make disappear from the stage. He was invited to perform this act on the steps of the White House. One time he brought back to Monmouth a pair of leopards, a python, 250 monkeys and 400 Chinese canaries, which he used in his huge mystic extravaganzas.

William Nicola, at age sixty-three, died at his Monmouth home on West First Avenue on February 1, 1946. At the time of his death he was survived by his widow, his brother Charles and his sister Maude Holt, all of Monmouth. The Great Nicola is buried in the Monmouth Cemetery.

Monmouth Sport and Musician

This past spring, "Tracking History" told of a former Monmouth High School student excelling in the state track meet. Jay Mayo "Inky" Williams put Monmouth High School on the map by winning the fifty-yard dash and finishing second in the one-hundred-yard dash during the 1912 Illinois state track meet at Champaign.

Little did we know then that this was just the beginning of the story.

J. Mayo Williams was born in Monmouth on July 25, 1894, was raised by his mother Millie and attended Prime Beef Center Schools through the eleventh grade. At this point, little is known of Williams's father. His mother remarried and they apparently moved to Chicago before his graduation from Monmouth High School.

Mayo Williams was a star football player for Monmouth during 1910, when they lost only one regular season game and played Rockford for the state championship. The Maroon and Gold (before being nicknamed the Zippers) held Keokuk, Rock Island and Kewanee scoreless. They topped off the regular season by thrashing Galesburg forty-nine to zero. The Monmouth yearbook described Williams as a player whose equal in dodging, speed, straight-arming, goal kicking, tackling and grabbing forward passes could not be found in the central states. It was further printed that those who had seen Williams play simply gasped in astonishment and were still wondering how he did it. During the 1911 season, Monmouth shut out visiting Galesburg nine to zero before a record-breaking crowd at Willard Field on the Knox College campus. Williams was the game's only scorer.

In 1917, Williams received a scholarship to attend the prestigious Brown University in Providence, Rhode Island. Williams was an outstanding end on the Brown University football team from 1917 through 1920, earning the *New York Times* Third Team All-American Honors his senior year. He also was a standout on the track team, being named New England champion of the forty-yard dash.

Williams joined Brown teammates Fritz Pollard and Bobby Marshall, who played for the University of Minnesota, as the first blacks to play in the American Professional Football Association. The APFA was the forerunner of the National Football League. Williams played professional football for six years with Canton, Hammond, Dayton and Cleveland. In the 1930s, he was football coach at Morehouse College in Atlanta.

Williams's life took an exciting turn following his pro football career when he became the first, and in his time the most successful, black executive in the U.S. recording industry. Williams produced records for some of the greatest blues artists of the twentieth century.

During his thirty-five years in the recording industry, Williams was best known for his production work for the Paramount, Brunswick, Vocalion and Decca labels. He later became owner of both Harlem Records out of New York and Ebony Records in Chicago. Williams produced and recorded for top blues artists Blind Boy Fuller, Blind Lemon Jefferson, Tampa Red, Louis Jordan, Ma Rainey and Muddy Waters.

Jay Mayo "Inky" Williams was indeed one of Monmouth's proudest sons. He passed away in Chicago on January 2, 1980, at the age of eighty-five.

AN AMUSEMENT LANDMARK

A case can be built that a former business located at 1721 North Henderson Street in the '50s and '60s may have touched as many lives as any local enterprise in history. Reliving the memories of an all-time favorite Galesburg amusement park is the most requested for this column. Tracking down data has been the most difficult of previous columns to date.

Thanks to the efforts of Sheryl Bacon and Patty Mosher, it seems fitting to remind area residents of the popular Kiddieland Amusement Park. Sheryl is the daughter of Saylor Conard, the last owner/operator of the fun park. Patty is the archivist at the Galesburg Public Library. Sheryl has donated a scrapbook of her Kiddieland memories, including pictures, to the library.

Legend is that in the early '50s a traveling carnival, whose owner went belly up financially while it was set up in Galesburg, abandoned the rides

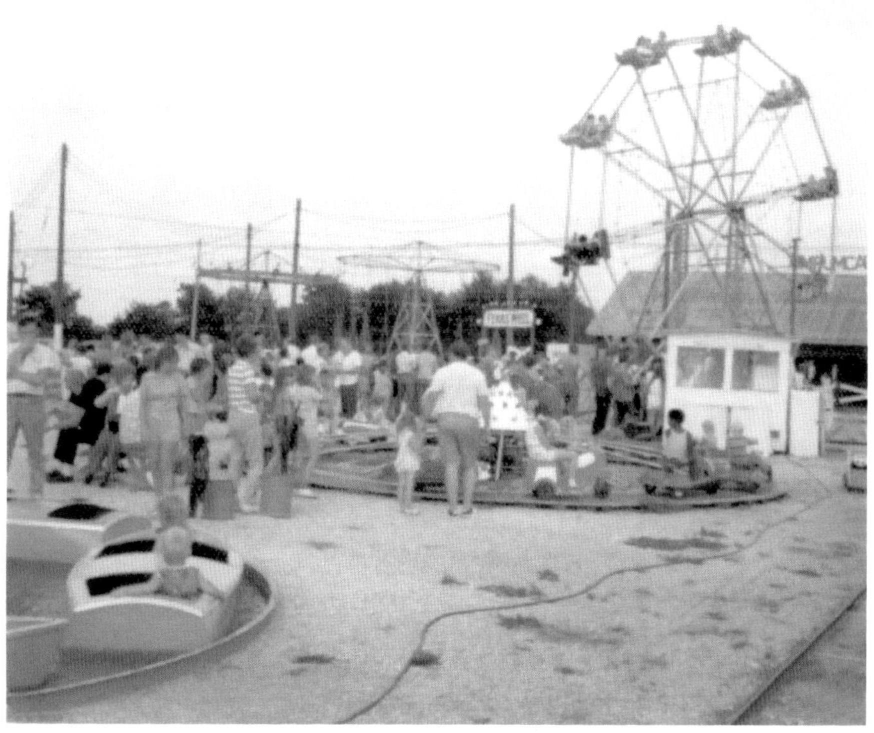

Kiddieland amusement park in Galesburg, 1971. The large Ferris wheel in the background was designed by former Galesburg resident George Washington Gale Ferris Jr. in the late 1890s. *Photo courtesy of Sheryl Conard Bacon.*

and flew the coop. Robert Green, known as the Traveling Welder, assumed ownership and operated the amusement park for nearly ten years. The answer to hundreds of area children's dreams included a Ferris wheel, merry-go-round, flying swings and the very popular bumper cars.

In 1962, Saylor Conard, his entire family and a multitude of his friends took over operation of Kiddieland. Conard's daughter remembered that her father's love for children was his motivation to keep the park alive. No child was ever left out, as free tickets were always available to those who couldn't afford them. Conard considered Kiddieland the vacation spot for those who couldn't afford the traditional vacation. The price per ride was maintained at ten cents until the later life of the operation.

The main marketing tool of Kiddieland was a giant beacon or searchlight that streamed a beam of light that circled the area skies. Many area youngsters would bug their parents to take them to the park when the giant

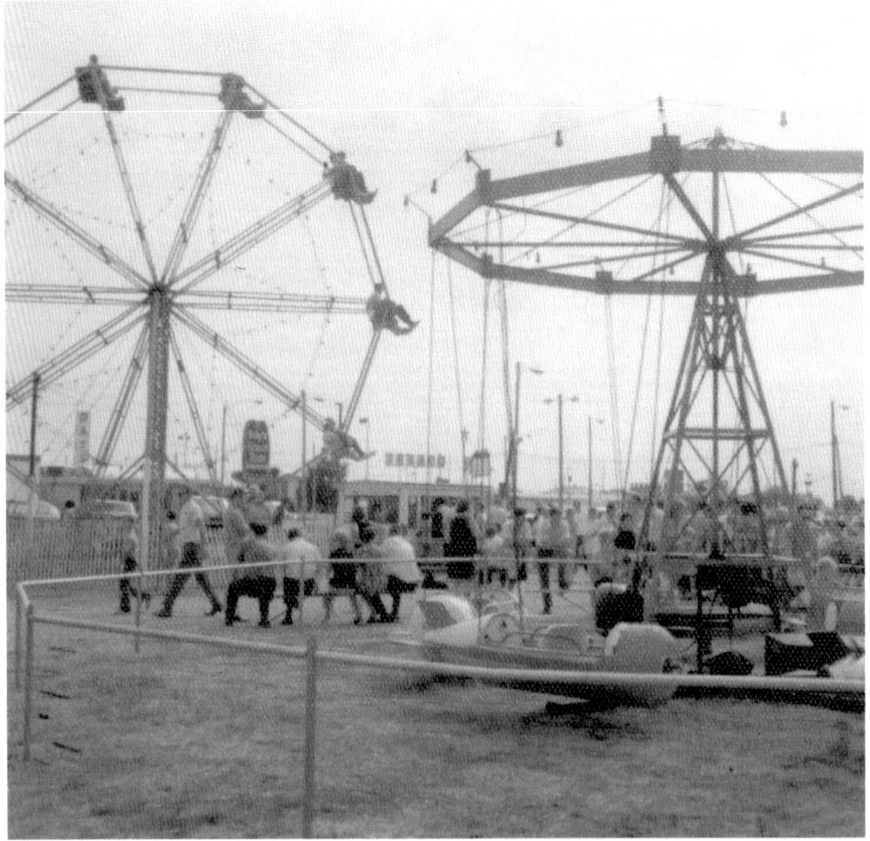

Galesburg Kiddieland amusement park, with a view of various children's rides, 1971. *Photo courtesy of Sheryl Conard Bacon.*

searchlight roamed the skies. Although it has not been confirmed, legend has it that the searchlight was the beacon from the Galesburg Airport south of Kiddieland on Henderson Street.

Kiddieland was for sure a family endeavor, with Saylor's wife, father and children selling tickets, running the train, repairing rides and selling delicious concession food. Concession fare included hot popcorn, snow cones, cotton candy and Green Rivers.

Much to both owners' credit, many middle-aged folks and teenagers were afforded needed jobs at the local amusement park. Jim Spellman and Ralph Plympton were two full-time employees who remained loyal until the very end. Other employees included Tom Hinton, Ted Gregory, Kenny Wixforth, Sharon Bainter, Christine Barton, Mary Louise Hinton, Cindy Dama and the Magnison guys.

Unfortunately, during mid-August 1972, the nearly twenty-year reign of Kiddieland came to a screeching halt. Soaring maintenance and rental costs forced Saylor Conard to turn out the lights for the final time. It was estimated that over one hundred cars carrying an average three kids visited the park daily; however, the effort to maintain the low ticket price of ten to fifteen cents made it impossible to cover expenses.

Many attempts were made to move the operations to the Lake Storey area and partner with the City of Galesburg. Although city officials were sympathetic to the cause, the city council repeatedly voted down the requested relocation. It was reported that a local bank had agreed to extend a loan if the city agreed to move the rides to Lake Storey. Over five thousand residents signed petitions urging the council to jump aboard. Members of the local Army Reserve unit volunteered to disassemble, move and reconstruct the rides if the new location was approved.

The soul of Kiddieland is long gone. The voices of joy from area children, the light in the sky and spinning rides are nowhere to be seen but will long be remembered.

Musicians Blessed Galesburg

Back in the early days of Galesburg theatre, vaudeville acts were the king of entertainment. Many famous musical entertainers performed at the Auditorium, Gala and Orpheum Theatres.

In the early days, the Orpheum pit orchestra was directed by DeWitt Depue. One of the prominent musical contributors who rattled out rhythms on the drums was Emmett Ronstrom of Galesburg. When the emergence of the silver screen and cans containing celluloid webs came to town and virtually killed vaudeville, Ronstrom, who was nicknamed "Slim," decided to take his talents to the big top circus world. After eight years with the Pollock Shrine Circus, Slim, then known as Rex, hit the big time and caught on with the famed Ringling Bros. and Barnum & Bailey Circus.

Emmett "Rex" Ronstrom was fortunate to be performing with Ringling Bros. Circus during the filming of Cecil B. DeMille's Oscar-winning movie, *The Greatest Show on Earth.* Rex retired from the circus life in 1954 and performed with the Oscar Babbitt Dixieland Band in Galesburg. Ronstroms's wife Kitty was instrumental in organizing Phi Beta, the national music and drama sorority at Knox College.

"Satchmo" blessed Galesburg! Famed jazz king Louis "Satchmo" Armstrong brought his six-piece band to the Galesburg High School

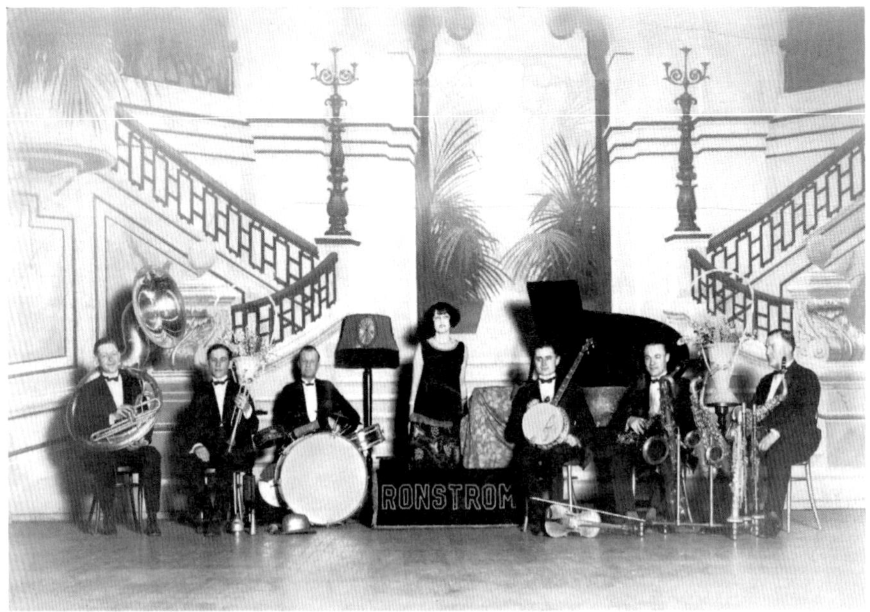

The Emmett Ronstrom Orchestra performing at the Galesburg Orpheum Theatre. Ronstrom, pictured playing drums, was a longtime performer with Ringling Bros. Circus.

auditorium during May 1961. The ambassador of jazz presented the sounds of the '30s through the '60s in his famed swinging style to a full house of delighted fans. Armstrong and his golden trumpet and gravel deep voice opened the concert with his signature song, "Sleepy Time Down South." Other favorites included "Old Man River," "Stompin at the Savoy," "Blueberry Hill," "Mack the Knife," "Yes Sir, That's My Baby" and "The Saints Go Marching In." It is interesting to note that Satchmo's fee to perform in Galesburg was $2,000.

"Champagne Music Maker Performs at Hill Arcade." Lawrence Welk and his Novelty Band entertained at the Arcade Roof Garden on July 16 and September 17, 1931. Galesburg's famed Roof Garden in the Weinberg Arcade was billed as "Where the Sky Begins" and offered twenty-five-cent admission and free dancing to "America's Biggest Little Orchestra." On September 18, 1931, the Arcade offered the "Big Battle of Music," featuring Lawrence Welk's Novelty Band and Vern Winter's Marigold Orchestra. It was billed as two outstanding orchestras and two floors of dancing.

As an interesting sidelight, it has been revealed that prior to one of Welk's appearances at the Roof Garden he sent a telegraph to Harlan Little, who

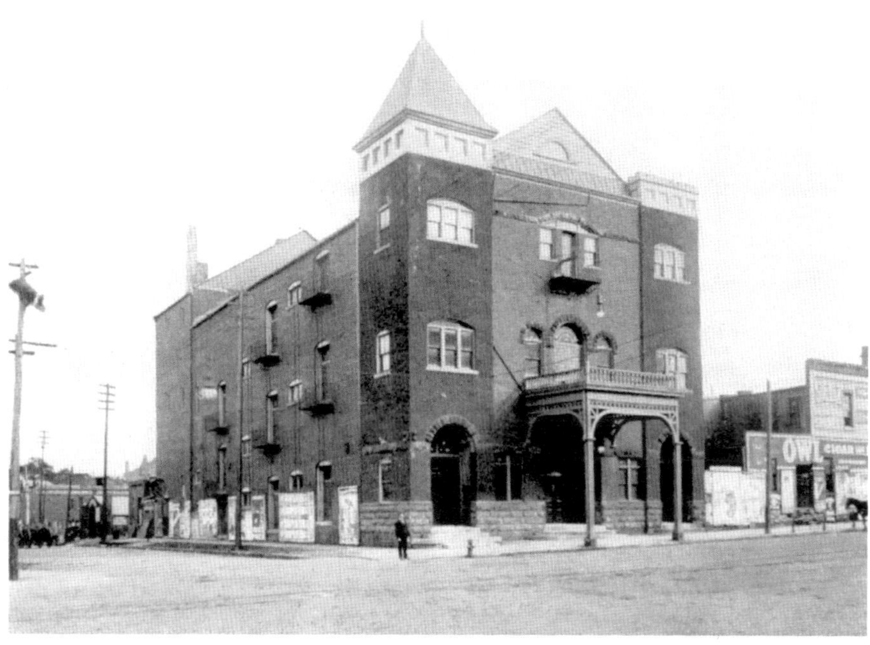

Galesburg Opera House during the late 1890s. The Marx Brothers were given their nicknames backstage at the Galesburg theatre during a poker game.

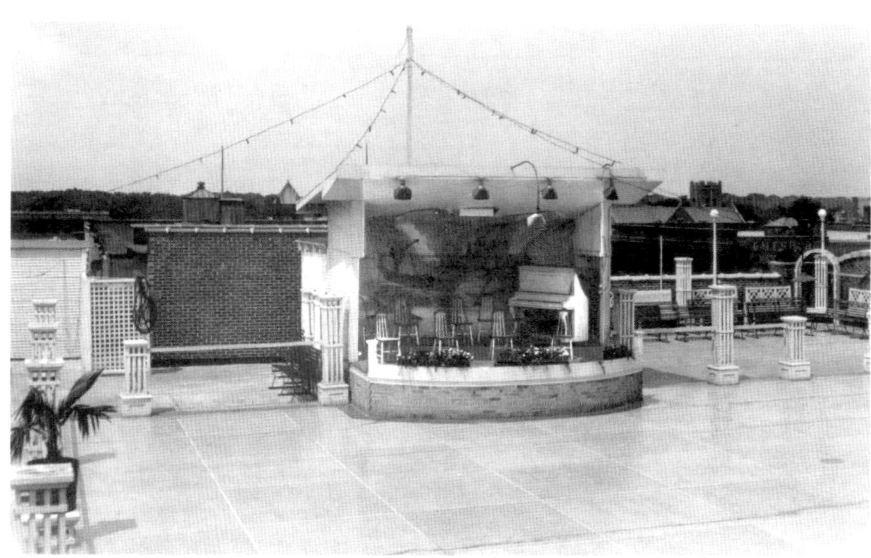

Weinberg Arcade Roof Garden dance emporium in Galesburg, 1929. Lawrence Welk and his band performed at the Roof Garden often.

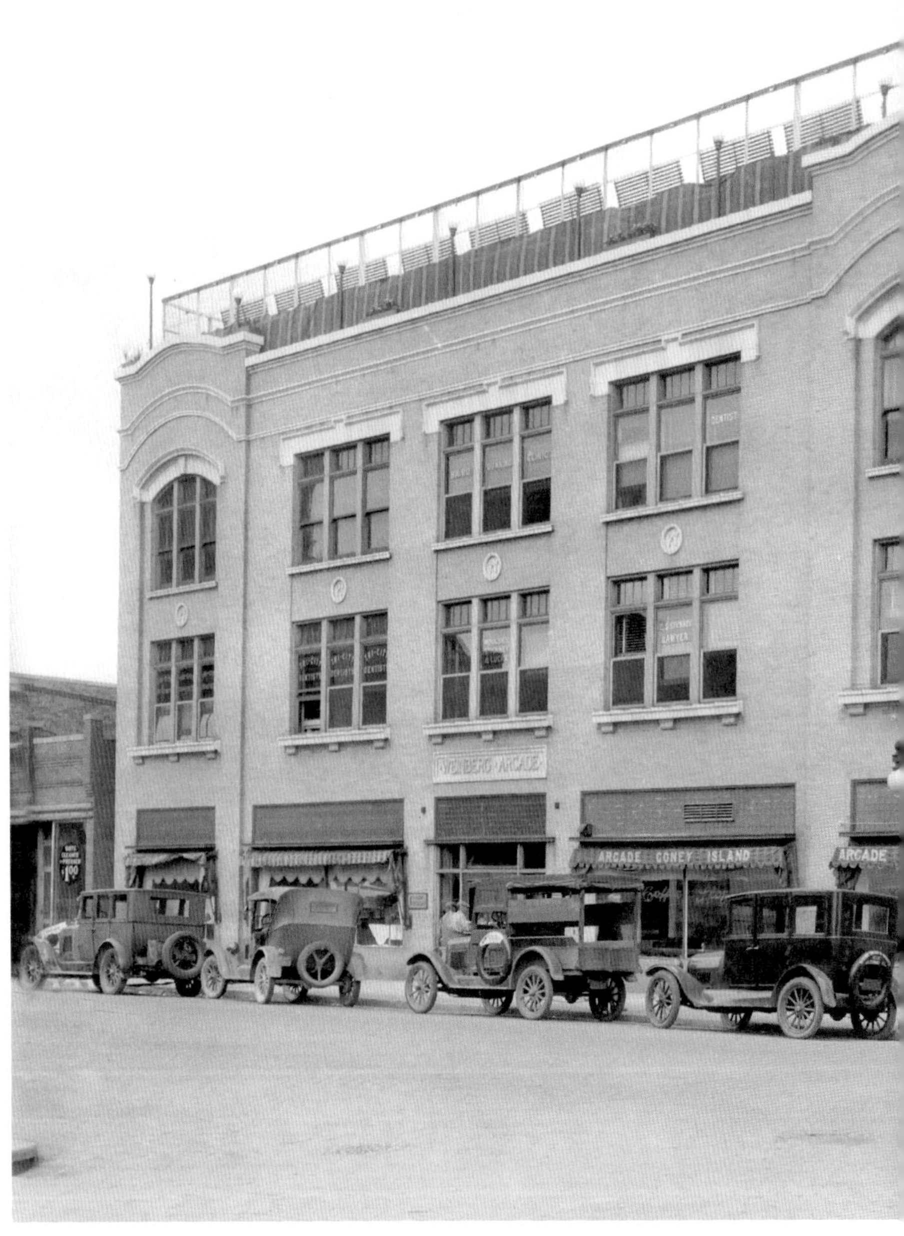

Exterior view of Galesburg Weinberg Arcade. The Arcade building contained the famous Roof Garden dance emporium on the top of the structure. Ronald Reagan danced at the Roof Garden often when he was a student at Eureka College.

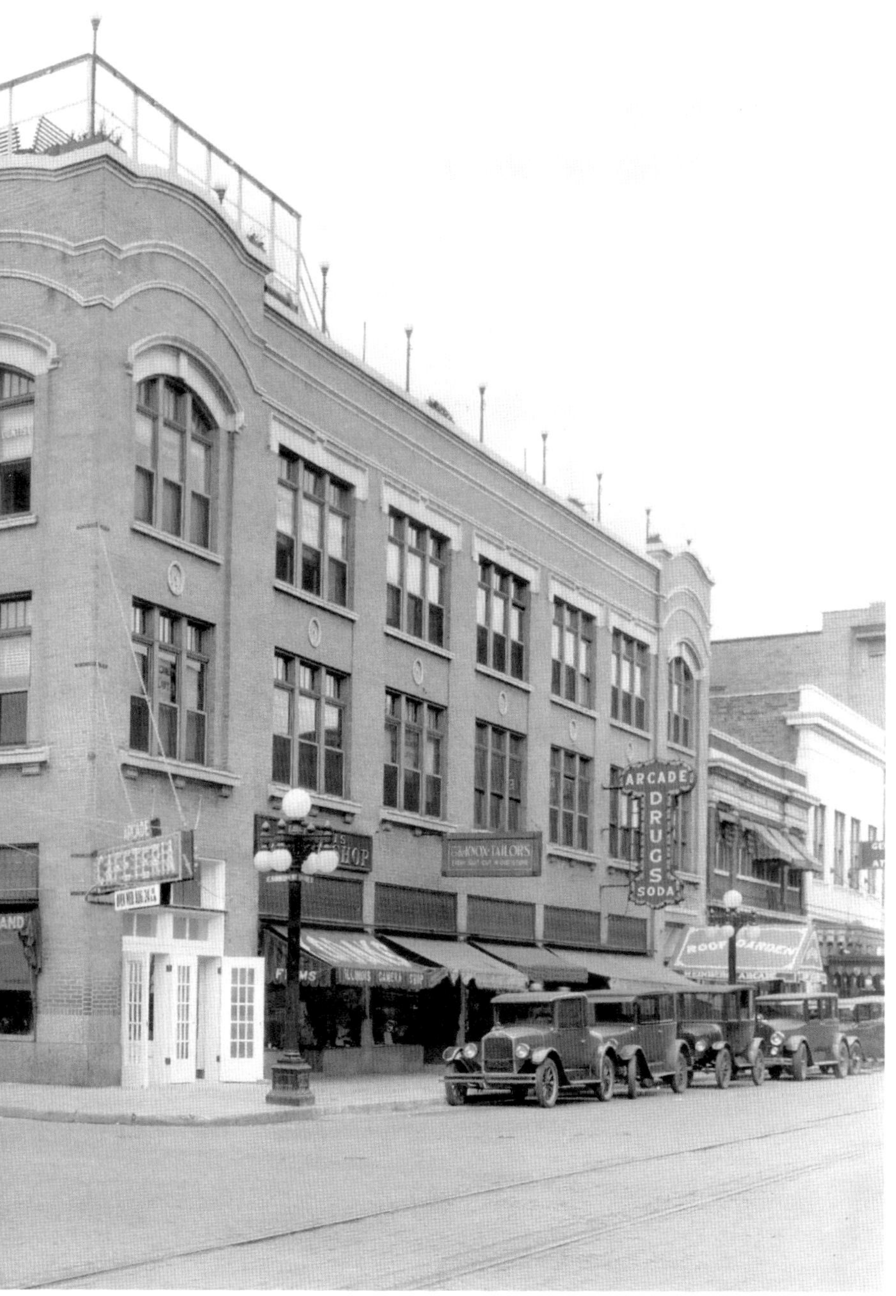
CAFETERIA
HOP
KNOX TAILORS
FILMS
ILLINOIS CAMERA SHOP
ARCADE
DRUGS
SODA
ROOF GARDEN

managed the Weinberg dance emporium, and requested an advance in funds. Welk told Little that he needed money for gas and meals for his band. The request was granted and Welk became a consistent performer "Where the Sky Begins"!